This Time Next Year

This Time
Next Year

A Life of Positive Thinking

DAVID JASON

CENTURY

1 3 5 7 9 10 8 6 4 2

Century
One, Embassy Gardens
8 Viaduct Gardens
Nine Elms
London SW11 7BW

Century is part of the Penguin Random House group of companies
whose addresses can be found at global.penguinrandomhouse.com.

Penguin
Random House
UK

First published by Century in 2024

www.penguin.co.uk

A CIP catalogue record for this book is available from the British Library.

ISBN (hardback): 9781529944198
ISBN (trade paperback): 9781529944204

Typeset in 13.25/17.5pt Goudy Oldstyle Std by Jouve (UK) Milton Keynes
Printed and bound in Great Britain by Clays Ltd, Elcograf S.p.A.

The authorised representative in the EEA is Penguin Random House Ireland,
Morrison Chambers, 32 Nassau Street, Dublin D02 YH68

www.greenpenguin.co.uk

MIX
Paper | Supporting
responsible forestry
FSC® C018179

Penguin Random House is committed to a
sustainable future for our business, our readers
and our planet. This book is made from Forest
Stewardship Council® certified paper.

*To all my loyal fans for their
encouraging support over the years*

CONTENTS

INTRODUCTION

Of time's rapid passing, artificial limbs and the path that lies ahead

This morning, shortly after rising, I stood in my robe at the window of my dressing room at Jason Towers and stared out across the grounds. The day seemed to find me in a thoughtful mood.

The autumn sunlight was illuminating the dew on the sloping lawns and glinting off the surface of the distant lake. Among the statues and the ancient cedar trees, a pair of squirrels fossicked eagerly, there being no law against that kind of thing for squirrels.*

Opening the casement, I was greeted by the tirelessly familiar symphony of English rural sounds: rooks calling to each other in the glade, wind stirring the whispery branches

---

* To fossick: verb, meaning to seek for precious items, especially by digging in the ground. Why, what did *you* think it meant? Actually, I don't think I want to know.

of the willow, and Timson the gardener firing up the leaf blower.

The scene was golden, but there was a distinct chill in the air, too. Winter was clearly on the way.

An idea crystallised in my head.

'I think I will take my coffee in the library this morning, Strobes,' I said, closing the window and turning to look across the room where my faithful retainer was applying the silver-handled clothes brush to one of my velvet smoking jackets. 'I feel another memoir coming on.'

'Very good, sir,' said Strobes. 'Then perhaps might I suggest that today we go with the *purple* cravat?'

'A most excellent selection, as usual, Strobes,' I replied, taking the proffered silk garment from Strobes's hand and attaching it to my neck at a raffish angle. 'So much more *writerly* than the yellow or the lilac, would you not agree?'

'I would, sir.'

And now here I sit, mid-morning, at my leather-topped desk in the quiet of the aforementioned library where the only sound, beyond the occasional pop and crackle from the freshly lit fire in the grate, is the soft scratching of my nib on the high-quality monogrammed writing paper in front of me.

Actually that's not quite the only sound. There's a slightly distracting kerfuffle coming from the shelves behind me where Daphne, the under-housemaid, is at the display cabinet, a Brasso-impregnated cloth clutched firmly in her hand, furiously buffing my BAFTAs.

Raising my head from the page, I turn and ask, with all the gentle patience I can muster, 'Will you be much longer, Daphne?'

'My apologies, sir,' Daphne replies, pausing and leaning back to wipe the sweat from her brow with her surprisingly well-muscled forearm. 'It's just that there are so many of them!'

'Ah, Daphne,' I reply, 'what can I say? Just the scarcely earned medals from my humble tour of duty at entertainment's front line . . .'

'No, but seriously, sir,' says Daphne, 'keeping your collection of awards polished . . . well, it's like the Forth Bridge, isn't it? No sooner is the Lifetime Achievement BAFTA at one end of the shelf all bright and shiny than the National Television Award from 2011 at the other end is looking all dull again! And as for the knighthood . . .'

At this point, naturally, I consider correcting Daphne on this well-intended misconception of hers. And, to be fair, it's a common one.

But the fact is, painting Edinburgh's Forth Bridge cannot accurately be said to be the definition of a never-ending task – or not any longer.

Yes, the first crew to climb up on that magnificent iron structure with the brushes and paint tins took three years to complete their work – by which time the end where they started was already going flaky again, so they walked back across and started again.

So, at that point, painting the Forth Bridge could indeed have been regarded as a job for life. One might even have been tempted to think of it as the decorating world's equivalent of clinching a major role on *Coronation Street*.

But that was back in the early years of the twentieth century. In 2002 the work became much more manageable with (and forgive me if I'm not telling you anything you don't already know here) the development of a more durable glass-based epoxy. Consequently nowadays the Forth Bridge only needs a lick of paint every quarter of a century or so, and restoring it is no longer the nice little earner it once was.

All of this I consider imparting to Daphne by way of enlightenment, and also with a view to supporting the cause of factual reality – an increasingly important battle, I feel, in this social media age of ours, when a falsehood can travel all the way round the world before truth has had the chance to get out of bed and put its socks on.

However, I decide that it would be a bit long-winded to get into all of that now, and that I have already been detained from my train of thought for long enough.

So instead I simply smile modestly and say, 'Daphne, really – you flatter me.

'And by the way,' I add, squinting over at the shelves, 'I think you've missed a bit. The nose on the BAFTA for Best Comedy Performance? Looks like it could use a further flap of the duster, no?'

'Lawks-a-lummy, sir, what am I like!' gasps Daphne,

quickly applying the cloth. 'Forgive me! I don't know where my head gets to sometimes!'

And, with another indulgent smile and a calming wave of the hand, I leave Daphne to her labours and return to the work in front of me.

The work in question being, of course, this book you are reading. If this is the first time you have joined me on one of these literary journeys, then welcome aboard and I'm very happy to have you along. As we set out together, you should immediately be reassured that no familiarity with my previously published *oeuvre* is presumed or required – though please do stop by the stall on your way out at the end, where the earlier volumes in this series and a selection of other highly desirable David Jason-branded merchandising will, I have no doubt, be made freely available to you by our friendly usherettes. (Well, when I say 'freely', I mean, obviously, at reasonable prices.)

If, on the other hand, you have passed this way before, and travelled with me already in the world of the printed word, then welcome back. Chances are you will be more or less familiar with the routine by now. In the pages ahead, I will, as ever, be updating you on the latest, hot-off-the-press developments in the daily life of this jobbing actor, who is relieved to find himself, thus far into his allotted span, still jobbing when the jobs can be found.

And at the same time I will be casting an eye backwards over my accumulated years in the cut and thrust of show business – lowering a bucket, if you will, into the deep well of my experience and then pulling it up again, full to the brim, hopefully, with tales of uplift and amusement, and perhaps, if we're lucky, with a lesson or two that we can carry onwards with us in our journeys.

And no doubt at some point I'll also dream up and throw in some fantastical tosh about Jason Towers and manservants and under-housemaids just for the heck of it. (Those bits of the book will be jokes, just so we're clear. Though you will never catch me complaining about the comfort in which I am fortunate enough to reside, here in deepest Buckinghamshire, I wouldn't want anyone forming the impression that it's anything like, for example, Sting's 865-acre Tuscan palace and winery. For one thing, we don't really have the climate for vineyards in the Aylesbury region. Or not yet, anyway.)

Up ahead, then, in the chapters to come, I will be inviting you to join me as I attempt to put my working life back in order after it was hit by a wrecking ball in the form of the pandemic; as I enjoy my eventual return to the nation's screens in *David & Jay's Touring Toolshed*; as I continue to wonder why, despite my very best efforts to attract the casting directors, Hollywood *still* hasn't come calling for me; and as I worry about the possible effect on my legacy if, as rumoured, the word 'plonker' falls into disuse.

You will also find me meditating on – in no particular order – actors' luxury trailers, my struggles with the concept of multi-tasking, and the peculiar place I seem to have taken up in the history of the chandelier.

I'll be describing in self-punishing detail the one night I spent as a stand-up comedian, which bears comparison with the one morning (much more recently) I spent as the operator of a kit-built drone. (Took it outside, flew it over a barn, crashed it in a ditch: end of drone.)

And I'll be flying to Florida in an attempt to escape, if only for a fortnight, the shadow of a certain Derek Trotter, who seems to follow me around wherever I go, for better and for worse.

I'll also write about a story you may have seen in the papers at the start of 2023, regarding the arrival in our family of a daughter and a grandson that I had no idea I had – an unexpected development, to say the least.

All these jewels, offered in my very best hand-tooled prose and interspersed with sundry flights of fancy and *jeux d'escargots* (as Del would no doubt call them), lie in store for you here, should you choose to stick around and go the distance.

If you detect a certain urgency in my desire to get these thoughts and stories down, I'm sure you'll understand why. Despite so many signals to the contrary (my lithe and surprisingly agile figure, my upright bearing, the sense of coiled energy that permanently emanates from me, like that of a jungle cat), I don't seem to be getting any younger. And, looking around me as I go about my business, I don't appear by any means to be alone in this. The clock ticks on, time makes its ravenous and not entirely welcome advances, and, so far as I can make out, not one of us has found a way to prevent it from doing so, with the sole exception of Cliff Richard.

(How does he do it? Cliff and I share a birth year, but I found myself quite close to him at a royal event not long ago, as you do, and I felt like I was being whisked off in the DeLorean from *Back to the Future*. The years seemed to be falling away from Cliff before my eyes. It was extremely impressive, and not a little envy-inducing.)

Of course, I am aware of the theory that age is just a number – that you are only as old as you feel, etc. I am equally aware how, in my own case, your age can seem completely unreal to you – something you don't really even believe. After a while, you start thinking, 'How could I possibly be this old? When did this happen? Where have these high numbers suddenly come from? And why have I been sent somebody else's birthday cards?'

I know what the reality is, obviously, but very often it seems to bear no relation to the way I think of myself at all. I'm still somewhere in my early forties, if you were to ask me to put a figure on it – or certainly as long as I stay away from mirrors. Naturally, then, I make a very determined effort to stay away from mirrors. (Gill, my dear wife, has sometimes suggested to me that this may be one of the reasons that I so often go out looking like I got dressed in the dark. She could have a point.)

So, yes, to a degree I suppose age is indeed just a number – an attitude, a frame of mind.

However, I also remember a moment from a Michael Parkinson show, many years ago now, when Yoko Ono, the artist and widow of John Lennon, was being interviewed, along with John Cleese. (This was not during my own appearance on *Parkinson* – we'll come to that later and to the topic of chat shows in general.) On this particular edition, Yoko was making exactly the point above – how age is really all in the mind and therefore, by extension, it's kind of up to us how old we are.

At which moment John Cleese, sounding as exasperated as only John Cleese can, interrupted and said something which, I think, rather cuts to the heart of this matter.

'But, Yoko, bits start dropping off!'

He had a point. Or bits certainly start wearing out. I speak as someone who, since last we met each other in the pages of a book, has had to have a new hip installed. One of the pair that I was originally issued with decided it had had enough and packed up on me. And I suppose I can't blame it, really, given the career I had put it through.

After all, much of that career was in theatrical entertainments, frequently of a farcical nature, which involved bouncing off beds and sofas and diving through serving hatches and landing offstage on unhelpfully thin crash mats, night after night and matinee after matinee, for years on end. Some part of me was bound to complain eventually.

Anyway, in response to those complaints, I ultimately sought medical advice and had my left hip replaced with a titanium one. This was in the autumn of 2023. I suppose it was thrilling to think that I was on my way to becoming Captain Scarlet and that parts of me hereafter would be officially indestructible. But the operation was, I confess, a pretty terrifying prospect, even though I knew I would be anaesthetised during the worst of it and therefore not around to listen to the hammering and the sawing and whatever else those doctors were going to be getting up to while I sweetly slumbered.

'Will I be able to play the trombone afterwards?' I asked the surgeon.

'Yes, absolutely,' he replied.

'Well, that's a bonus,' I said, 'because I've always wanted to be able to.'

'You'll be uncomfortable for a while,' the surgeon also warned me. He wasn't kidding. When I came round from the op, I felt like I'd been the site of an archaeological excavation during which they had extracted three intact mosaic floors and a selection of gold drinking artefacts which entirely changed historians' understanding of how people lived in Roman Britain.

I was bruised like a boxer and stitched up like a tapestry.

For days afterwards I couldn't sleep properly because every time I turned over onto that side, or even thought about doing so, the pain in the affected area would set an alarm bell clanging throughout the rest of my body and I'd wake up.

Still, I gritted my teeth and persevered, dutifully complying with the physio rehab exercises to help my titanium joint get settled into its new home. And then, when it was strong enough, I advanced to the next stage of the programme, which involved, among other things, cycling on a static bike.

Now, gym work has never been my idea of a fun time, and the last time I was on a bicycle was probably while playing Granville in *Still Open All Hours*, for which, of course, I was paid. But needs must.

However, not for me one of those fancy Peloton machines with a computer screen bolted to the handlebars – oh no. Those things are pricey. You could get a decent second-hand car for the money they seem to ask for the posher kind of exercise bike, and actually go somewhere in it. Also, though I know other people swear by this kind of thing, I didn't especially fancy having a virtual instructor shouting 'You can do this!' and 'Go for the burn!' at me while I worked out. I'm not sure it would have brought out the best in me. 'Go for your *own* burn!' I would have been tempted to shout back. And other things.

So instead I went for the home-made option, rigging up Gill's old bike on a frame. A fully non-digital exercise apparatus! Out I would go to the garage every morning, where I would saddle up and pedal away grimly, going nowhere but getting fitter.

And very soon I was restored and back in action – and even quietly considering a tilt at the Tour de France, where at least I'd have some scenery to look at while I cycled, rather than the garage wall, of which I had grown somewhat bored.

I also, in this rehab period, became quite adept at bouncing on a mini-trampoline. Again, I don't know about you, but trampolining is not something I have found much time for in recent years, and I can't pretend I went at it hard enough in these particular sessions to reach what anyone might regard as Olympic standard. Certainly, if I'm being absolutely honest, my tucked one-and-a-quarter front somersault with a full twist still needed a little polishing by the end of the programme. However, I'm sure the bouncing that I did manage to pull off aided my swift recovery. And, for a bonus, I now have some valuable skills under my belt in the event that I ever run away and join a circus.

Anyway, having been the recipient of many kind notes of concern and best wishes in advance of this procedure, I thought I had better make some kind of public declaration of my return to health. So, with the help of Gill and her iPhone, I recorded a video message for release through the digital portals of the tirelessly loyal *Only Fools and Horses* Appreciation Society.

Filmed one sunny morning on location in my backyard, and with no expense spared, this surely BAFTA-worthy clip featured me entering stage right in the middle distance, meekly limping along, hunched over the pair of crutches which (apart from the static bike) had been my chief mode of transport for the previous month or so.

It would have been clear to anyone who saw these heart-rending images that I was but a shrivelled husk of the man I used to be – a really quite pitiful sight.

But then, turning and pausing, I stood slowly upright, extending to the full height of my famously imposing frame, and, in a transformation which could only be described as miraculous, flung my crutches away and advanced upon the camera with the easy sashay of a man of international jet-set pleasure, before concluding with a flurry of shadow-boxing just to show exactly how up-and-at-'em I was.

And then I went to have a little sit-down and get my breath back, but we didn't film that bit.

Still, that was my hip surgery well and truly overcome, and I was once more ready to bob and weave my way around life's boxing ring with a titanium-powered spring in my step. Happy days!

Except, of course, as I am rapidly learning about the ageing process, the absence of niggling pain of some kind, some-where in your body, is only ever temporary. There's usually something having a go. It's as if the pain migrates around your body – sets up camp in one place, then gets bored and heads off somewhere else.

At the moment, for example, as I write this, the pain is

enjoying a week's holiday in my lower back. And after that, I've no doubt, it will probably be thinking about popping up to my shoulder for a few days or maybe dropping in on one of my knees to see how everybody is down there.

Actually, this particular bout of back pain is my fault. It's the result of me foolishly overextending myself one recent weekend.

And how, you will ask, did I cause this really quite extensive discomfort, with branch lines now extending all the way down one leg? Was it while taking an ill-advised Harley-Davidson motorbike ride through the Chilterns? Was it during a dawn kick-boxing session with my personal trainer? Was it while winning a hotly contested axe-throwing contest over the course of a 'wild man' camping weekend in Thetford Forest?

No, it was none of these. It was on a Sunday afternoon at home while lightly weeding a raised flower border.

I know – it's humiliating, isn't it? The thespian athlete who once effortlessly dangled from the scenery on a West End stage in his boxer shorts, and never seemed to pay the price for it afterwards, is now reduced to a groaning wreck by half an hour of gardening.

Worse than that – *seated* gardening.

But that was the problem, in fact. Rather than operate from a standing position, I chose to park myself on the edge of this raised border and do my weeding from there. Taking the weight off my feet for a while seemed to make sense at the time. But turning to get at the weeds caused me to adopt a slightly twisted posture, which, over a period of time, my back – still not quite over the shock of having a new hip move into the neighbourhood – was clearly not very happy about. Next morning I was hobbling about the place and wincing like someone who had just been sawn in half by an under-rehearsed magician.

Once more unto the physiotherapist, then. The one I'm lucky enough to see used to work (and I'm not making this up) with the England rugby team. Consulting him over my latest ailment, I asked him in passing if he'd seen many gardening-related injuries during his time fine-tuning the muscles and bones of international rugby's elite.

He didn't especially surprise me when he admitted that he hadn't.

Ah, the indignities of age! Crippled by weeding! Still, at the present juncture, I can at least blessedly state that my mental faculties remain intact, and while that's the case there is much to be grateful for. Why, I can't even remember the last time I went upstairs to get something and then forgot what it was. So, on we go.

All of which leads me to the title of this book, and my broader purpose here, in as much as I have one. This time next year . . . Those words – the text for our sermon, if I may put it that way – will, I feel pretty confident, be familiar to you from *Only Fools and Horses* where, for Del, they formed the first part of what quickly became a catchphrase.

'This time next year, Rodney, we'll be millionaires.'

Most often, of course, the line expressed Del's uncrushable optimism, deployed tactically to drag his younger brother down the path with him on whichever hare-brained scheme Del happened to have got into his head at the time – second-hand motors, chandelier cleaning, 'ethnic' bus tours of London (all the great sights: Lower Edmonton by night, the Post Office sorting depot at Mount Pleasant) . . .

Sometimes, though, Del used the phrase as a little nugget of inspiration for someone else – like, for instance, Alex, the struggling travel agent, to whom Del offers his 'next customer gets the biggest cut-price holiday in the history of travel' gimmick in order to stimulate trade.

Del tells Alex, 'This time next year, you'll be a millionaire.'

Needless to say, it doesn't work out that way. But it's the thought that counts.

And just occasionally Del was clearly using the phrase to pick *himself* up. That was certainly the case in 'A Losing Streak' in the second series, during the big poker game scene between Del and Boycie.

Del at this point is troubled by some teetering debts, but he doesn't want the others to know that he's troubled. Plus he's got a genuine mink coat (colour: tabby) and a pile of knocked-off bottles of 'parfum de toilette' to sell at the market, so there's room to be positive, even though things seem to be heavily stacked against him.

So, when Rodney asks him if he's all right, Del replies that nothing's wrong at all, that he's never better in fact, and that, yes, 'this time next year we'll be *millionaires*'.

The point is, no matter how bad life gets, for himself or for others, Del can always manage to keep a flicker of optimism alight. He never turns inward, or not for long. Things might look terrible, but, as far as Derek Trotter is concerned – and even in the face of constant evidence to the contrary – the future can be relied upon to deliver.

This is the spirit that that extraordinary character created by the writer John Sullivan embodies, and one of the reasons, I think, why people tend to like him so much. Whoever we are (almost), at some level we relate to him. His life is a catalogue of humiliations and disasters on various scales, from small to large, but he continues to believe in himself and he continues to strive. He falls through life's bar flap, but he's up again in the next shot and dusting himself down and flexing his neck and trying to make it look as though the fall never happened.

The past is gone, he tells us, and can't be fixed. The only thing you are in a position to work with is the future. In the loveliest way, and without his feet ever floating too far off the ground, Derek Trotter carries the flag high for staying positive and ploughing on for as long as you possibly can, and something in us recognises something lovely in that which we wouldn't mind having for ourselves, and goes along with him.

It's why, I guess, all these years after the show was made,

17

Del continues to occupy the place that he does in the culture. And maybe we could use an extra bit of his spirit at the moment. It's hard not to feel that the world has been darkening around us somewhat of late – and that's not just my eyesight going. (My eyesight is actually pin-sharp, thank you for asking.)

War and destruction, anger and division, climate change, soaring prices, politicians who don't seem to be quite the ticket . . . A whole horde of things seems to have come along in a cluster to dampen our mood. Or, as Del notes, in a moment of philosophical reflection: 'One minute you're walking along quite nicely, and the next minute, whack! Life jumps out and gives you sobering thoughts.'

And as Grandad chips in: sobering thoughts were what started him drinking. Which, of course, is not to be recommended . . .

So consider that, if you will, to be the humble mission guiding this collection of updates and tales from this very lucky actor's life: to provide a bit of distraction from the sobering thoughts that life keeps jumping out to give us. And to offer a little gentle guidance, in as much as I am able to provide it, regarding the whacks and how to walk on after them.

Without further ado, then, let's pick up from where I left off last time – which, as I recall, was with me face down on the bedroom floor, life having jumped out and whacked me good and proper . . .

CHAPTER ONE

Of lockdowns, mentors and the shop that couldn't close

My mistake that time, I now realise, was to assume that I could make the journey from my bed to the bathroom. And, in fairness to myself, why wouldn't I have thought that? It wasn't as though it was a mission I had never completed before.

On the contrary. I knew the terrain very well – the ups and downs, the ins and outs, the tricky corners. Why, I could have made that journey in the dark – and did so most nights, in fact, often a couple of times.

And on this occasion I was going to be doing it in broad daylight. So, a piece of cake, surely.

The difference was that up to now I'd been making the trip uninfected by Covid. The dreaded virus had packed me off to bed a couple of days before this, with the 'flu-like' symptoms which all of us very quickly learned to call 'typical' – a cough, shortness of breath, exhaustion, etc.

But unbeknown to me, while I'd been lying there, feeling sorry for myself, Covid had also decided it might be amusing to take all the strength out of my lower limbs – a bit like a kid sucking the last bits of a milkshake out of a carton with a straw, but secretly and without the giveaway slurping noises.

Consequently, one moment I was rising confidently from the sheets – bathroom-bound, a man with a purpose. The next I was face down on the carpet and unable to get up.

Now, I'm as fond of a comedy pratfall as the next person. Dear reader, I've even, I might humbly mention, attempted a few in my time, in search of the sweet music which is an audience's tinkling laughter. But even if my life had taken a different direction and I had never had cause to fall over in a professional capacity, I would appreciate that somebody taking a tumble is frequently funny, certainly if it's done well.

And somebody tripping and *not* falling over is *always* funny. That's just one of humour's founding laws. Certainly the history of comedy would be an awful lot shorter if you took out all the bits in which humans come a cropper. Finding this kind of thing amusing may, indeed, be one of those things that separates us from the animals, who don't tend to fall over anywhere near as much as we do, nor laugh about it all that frequently when it happens.

However, on this occasion, down there on the bedroom floor, any amusement that I might have been able to muster was quickly eclipsed by other feelings, including, I must admit, fright. There seemed to be a number of genuinely alarming things to consider in that moment, beyond comedy.

First of all, why weren't my muscles working any more – and did they have any plans to resume work any time soon? Or, indeed, ever?

And secondly, given that my muscles weren't working any more, how was I going to get up?

And thirdly, given that my muscles weren't working any more and I had a mouthful of carpet, how was I going to attract the attention and assistance of my wife, Covid-free and carefully isolating elsewhere in the house?

I've written about them before, so I won't dwell too long here on the contortions which occupied the ensuing minutes – the struggle during which, without functioning arms or legs to help me, I tried to row my body in the direction of the door using my forehead as an oar.

Suffice it to say there was one main lesson I learned during this protracted struggle: your forehead is not intended to be used as an oar.

By the time my wife had heard my muffled noises of distress – plus, of course, the muffled noises of my face dragging along the floor – and had burst through the door in a state of alarm, I was several feet across the room, heading in a roughly easterly direction, and with carpet burns stretching from my hairline to the tip of my nose.

I think back wonderingly to the picture the two of us must have presented at that bleak moment. There was me, with a grazed beak, stretched out pathetically on the floor; and there was Gill in her improvised PPE – two face masks, a pair of surgical gloves and a *Better Call Saul*-branded onesie with the hood pulled over her head. Remembered from this distance, this whole scene has the flavour of a bizarre dream, like so much of that extraordinary and puzzling period in all our lives.

That was in the summer of 2022. The worst of the pandemic was technically over at that point. Freed from the shackles which had descended on us all, the world was getting back to normal, or something like it. And I looked like seeing out this challenging spell as one of the fortunate ones – entirely untouched by the bug.

For two and a half years, the virus had been out there, looking for me. And for the whole of that time I had escaped its clutches, using all the tricks I had learned in my years working undercover in elite-level espionage.*

I changed my routines to confuse it. Whenever I went out, I did so in disguise – with a mask over my face. I kept it at a distance – two metres generally, in accordance with the recommendations. I took special potions to make myself invisible – or, at least, I got the vaccine and the boosters.

---

* By which I mean the period between 1981 and 1992, when, for ten series and eighty-nine episodes, I had the honour of providing the voice of Danger Mouse, the cartoon British Secret Service operative working out of a red pillar box on Baker Street. Say what you like about my espionage experience, I learned from the best.

And it was all working. I seemed to be getting away scot-free.

But it reached me in the end, as it reached so many of us. I got Covid unfashionably late, but when I did, I got it good and proper. And, as I lay and gradually recovered from that episode on the floor, it led me to a fuller understanding of exactly how powerfully that virus could operate, when it had a mind to – and how lucky I had been to be on the right side of the vaccination programme, and therefore bolstered against it, when it finally chose to visit me. You will quite likely know people who were less lucky. And if you do, you have my sympathy.

As soon as my strength fully returned, which took a while, I was back on my feet and looking forward to work returning, too. I don't know about you, but I found lockdown extremely difficult to cope with. Being occupied has always suited me far better than being unoccupied. And during that period, in the place where work had been, there was nothing, unless you count staring mournfully out of the window and sighing quite a lot.

I think one of the reasons that the emptiness of that period sent a shiver down my spine was that it felt like a dry run for retirement. For many of us in the acting trade, retirement is something that happens to us despite ourselves, when the work dries up. Actors don't retire, in the main. They get retired – by producers and by casting directors and, beyond them, of course, by the public, who sit in ultimate judgement on what you do. These will be the people eventually telling you that the time has come and that you are now surplus to requirements. And accordingly, because retirement is outside our control, it's a truly chilly prospect for nearly everyone in my trade.

Mostly we actors spend our lives dreaming of the next role that's going to turn up and wondering whether *that's* going to be the big one, the one that *really* makes the world sit up and listen. That's the habitual mindset of the jobbing actor, almost irrespective of what stage you are at in your career, and it's a hard habit to shake once you've acquired it.

Consequently I've met vanishingly few professional thespians who have decided, off their own bat, to retire – to draw a line under it all and walk off into the sunset clutching the gold carriage clock and the best wishes of their still active peers. Rare is the actor who isn't, in some part of their mind, however small, entertaining the hope of future work, even if they aren't necessarily saying as much out loud.

Now, one striking exception to the rule was my old pal Ronnie Barker. Ronnie, entirely of his own volition, began his retirement promptly on New Year's Day 1988. It didn't happen arbitrarily, either. It was thoroughly planned in advance. He'd set the date two years earlier, and told only a handful of people about it.

I was really disappointed when I heard the plan because I felt it was far too soon for a man of Ronnie's talents to be stepping down. Ronnie said, 'No one wants to see a seventy-year-old on television who can't remember his lines.' But Ronnie *wasn't* seventy. He was only fifty-nine. He wasn't merely proposing retiring, he was proposing taking *early* retirement.

But there was nothing I or anyone else could do or say to change his mind. He was adamant and it was hard to challenge him on it because I knew he had his own personal reasons for being so. Put bluntly, he feared the work might one day kill him.

Two of Ronnie's peers had recently suffered heart attacks and died while working in theatres. In 1984, Eric Morecambe, who had been beset by problems with his heart for some time, had taken part in a charity show at the Roses Theatre in Tewkesbury and collapsed in the wings as he came off after the curtain calls. He died in hospital that night.

Then, just a few months later, Leonard Rossiter collapsed and died while waiting to go on stage at the Lyric Theatre in London to appear in the Joe Orton play *Loot*. Leonard was fifty-seven and Eric was fifty-eight – no age at all. The nature and timing of those deaths affected Ronnie profoundly. And don't forget that they came on top of the death of the exceptionally talented Richard Beckinsale, Ronnie's co-star in *Porridge*, who suffered a heart attack at home one weekend in 1979, at the age of just thirty-one. It took us all a long time to get over the shock and sadness of that.

But in addition to grief, Ronnie felt that all these losses

were warnings to him. So, he withdrew and spent the next ten years very happily tending to his house and his garden and his antique shop, the Emporium, in the Cotswolds.

Except that even Ronnie was tempted out of the garden eventually. He made a couple of television appearances with Ronnie Corbett, presenting *Two Ronnies* tribute programmes. And then, in 2002, aged seventy-three, he played the part of Winston Churchill's butler in a drama for the BBC, *The Gathering Storm*, before, a year later, taking a role alongside the great Maggie Smith in a TV movie, *My House in Umbria*.

And yes, he was seventy-plus by the time he made those appearances, but he didn't forget his lines or even look like doing so, and people were very happy to see him. Very happy, too, to be reminded of the extent to which Ronnie was an actor as much as he was a comic. And clearly the acting bug had not left him. For those of us who get bitten by it, I'm not sure it ever does.

Incidentally, on the subject of Ronnie's skills as an actor, you may not know that the show *The Fall and Rise of Reginald Perrin*, from the David Nobbs novel, was originally planned to be a two-part drama. And in the role of Reggie Perrin was going to be not Leonard Rossiter as eventually happened but . . . Ronnie Barker.

Then the plan changed and the show became a sitcom. David Nobbs tells a story about meeting the BBC's head of comedy at that point and being asked who he had in mind for the title role.

'Ronnie Barker,' David said.

'Right,' said the head of comedy. 'Leonard Rossiter it is, then.'

And thus do casting decisions get made.

Anyway, I digress. The point is, retirement is a dirty word for most of us acting types, but in 2020 the pandemic made retired people of us all. With productions postponed or cancelled and everything frozen, I suddenly found myself flicking through a painfully empty diary – page after page of days stretching ahead in which I had nothing to fill my time except golf.

And the problem with that was I don't even play golf. And the courses were shut anyway.

So what did I have to fill those idle hours, if I didn't have golf? Well, I had making tomato chutney, I suppose. Before lockdown, that was one of the things that happily filled a few of my days off. But could I eventually expand it to fill *all* of my days? That was the question lockdown seemed to be asking.

And the answer to that question seemed to me, quite quickly, as the jars of chutney mounted up in the kitchen, to be 'not really, no'. It turns out there's a limit to how much tomato chutney anyone needs.

And I've a shipment of a couple of tons of the condiment still bottled up and waiting to move out, if anyone's interested. Decent stuff, and you won't eat a better tomato chutney this side of the next pandemic. Let me know.

Model-making – that was another time-filler. I decided to occupy my twiddling thumbs by building things. Again, this was something I had always liked to do during time off – repairing and restoring old slot machines in particular. I love those machines that have an animated element in them – love getting into the mechanics of all of that. Maybe making animated models could fill the much bigger gap that was now available.

So I sent off for a kit and made it. Then I sent off for another one and made that. And then I sent off for another one. Model-making very quickly grew to be quite addictive. My table started to fill up with the products of these labours: a six-inch-high wooden man playing a trumpet; a slightly smaller figure rowing a boat; a wooden traction engine with a wooden engine driver . . . all with their own little animated elements.

On it went. I could sense my wife beginning to cast a wary eye. It was like I was creating a kit-built version of the Terracotta Army in there. If lockdown went on much longer, the entire house would be occupied by finely detailed men operating various modes of transport or musical instruments. Then, quite possibly, they would rise up and take over one night, and we would have no alternative but to hand the place over to them and go and live in the garden.

Things may have reached a literal tipping point with the fully operational ball chute. That one was, let me tell you, a real challenge to build – an intricate miniature obstacle course, a kind of Heath Robinson contraption, through which a small steel ball could be made to wend its way.*

Give me credit for patience, though. Sitting back after my long hours of intricate labour, and sending that little ball down on its first run, I was filled with pride at what I had created. Well, for a little while, anyway. After a couple more runs, the novelty wore off and I moved on to the next model.

Well, it's the journey, I always say, not the arrival. And I normally mean it in relation to one's passage through life: worry less about conceiving some big goal for yourself, and take your pleasures instead in the immediate work along the way. That approach has always seemed a wise one to me, and it hasn't served me badly with acting through the years.

But it applies to most things, I would suggest. And it definitely applies to model-making. Model-making is *all* about

---

* I hope the name of W. Heath Robinson is familiar to you, but just in case it's not, he was a cartoonist who, in the first half of the twentieth century, drew fantastical machines and devices which all provided ludicrously elaborate ways to do simple things. Hence the 'multi-movement tabby silencer', a machine that could spray water over noisy cats, the preposterous and self-explanatory 'head-wart remover', and the 'anti-litter machine', which somehow needed to incorporate a car, a teetering lookout tower and a massive sticky drum from which the driver could eventually remove the gathered scrap of litter with a toasting fork before depositing it in the bucket behind him. Heath Robinson is the patron saint of mechanical pointlessness and I frequently felt his presence hovering at my shoulder during the most intense moments of my lockdown model-building phase.

the journey, I'm here to tell you, having made many, many such journeys during lockdown.

And then there was my excursion into making riding-boot lamps. What's a riding-boot lamp? It's a lamp, made from a riding boot. What else did you think it could be?

And trust me, it's a thing. You'll see them on American websites going for $800 a time. Well, that's the price tag on them, anyway. Whether anyone actually *pays* $800 for them is another matter.

Anyway, I made six of them – half a dozen riding-boot lamps. I found three pairs of old riding boots, left behind by the previous owners of the house, made moulded wooden inserts for them, kitted them out with light fittings and wired them up. Then I added a shade, polished them and gave them a finishing coat of dubbin. Hey presto – an elegant and practical ornamental addition to any home, and a guaranteed conversation starter.

'Is that lamp actually a riding boot?'

'Now, it's funny you should say that . . .'

Still, half a dozen of them was probably more riding-boot lamps than we strictly needed. My wife thought so, definitely. My daughter Sophie offered to flog them for me online, which seemed like a good idea, although then there would be her commission to consider, which was going to eat into the profits a bit. And I was already in for the price of the brass lamp fittings and the shades, the wiring and the plugs. If I wasn't careful I'd be selling for cost, or worse.

The business idea faded. The riding-boot lamps are currently sitting together in the workshop, waiting for . . . I'm not sure what. Christmas maybe.*

All in all, I think you will probably agree that, after a year and a half of this kind of thing, work could not return to take its place in my life soon enough. Even the dogs had started looking slightly anxious about my constant company. Initially they had seem quite pleased that I was suddenly always around and permanently available for consultation on the things that matter to them, such as food, walks and food. But later I'd catch them giving me looks across the room that seemed to say, 'No plans again?'

And there was nothing I could really do except look back at them, shrug, and say with a sigh: 'Nope. No plans.'

There had been a couple of projects in particular that I was looking forward to starting in on before the pandemic intervened and skittled everything. One of them was a small role in a film – but I had learned to lower my expectations of film roles ever coming to anything, for reasons which I'll talk about later, so it wasn't too hard to let that one linger in the ether for a little while longer. Indeed, if the precedents were anything to go by, it would probably end up lingering in the ether forever.

---

* Again, if you know anyone who's in the market for one, get in touch. $800 a throw to you. Or $2,000 the pair. Can't say fairer. What are you waiting for? You know it makes sense.

But the other project was a new series of *Still Open All Hours* for the BBC, which was, for obvious reasons, a more solid proposition. And the postponement of that project really *did* cause me some disappointment – and even more so when that postponement then turned into a cancellation.

I loved doing *Still Open All Hours*, just as I had loved doing *Open All Hours*, the original series with Ronnie Barker back in the 1970s and 80s. Some characters you play stay with you long after you've stopped playing them, and I suddenly had this thought one day: I wonder what Granville would be doing now?

Would he have inherited his departed Uncle Arkwright's corner shop? Would he be keeping it going – maybe even keeping Arkwright's spirit alive? Would he be any further along the road to finding contentment in his love life? Would any of the old customers still be knocking around? There seemed to me to be so many rich routes that story could go down.

With the encouragement of Mark Freeland, the then Head of Comedy at the BBC, I took that idea to the show's writer, Roy Clarke, who converted it into words and stories. To see that show get made and broadcast on national television – in 2013 initially – brought me a lot of satisfaction and pride.

Some people accused the show of being old-fashioned, but it was *meant* to be old-fashioned. That was the point of it. It harked back to an old programme, and to people's memories of that programme, and it was intended to be the kind of early-evening sitcom that doesn't get made very often now-adays but which some people still love to watch and for which I firmly believe there is still a space. The fact we ran for six series over the next six years seems to back me up on that.

The BBC had commissioned a seventh series of the show in 2019, and by the end of the year Roy Clarke had written all six episodes for it. I thought they were brilliant. They were going to bring the story to a close. They were going to see Granville finally married to the ever-hesitant 'Wavy Mavy' – Maggie Ollerenshaw's Mavis. It all seemed like a very fitting and highly satisfying resolution – a lovely note for the show to end on. Everything was set to go, with filming scheduled for the spring and summer of 2020, and I couldn't wait to get cracking.

But then, of course, along came Covid and the project got postponed and I ended up making a model of a man in a rowing boat instead.

Also a Saturn V rocket. And a wooden cityscape with a working big wheel and boats bobbing on water.

By the time the pandemic had cleared off, I was absolutely desperate to get on and make that show. But days and weeks went past, and the call never came. What had happened to our commission? There followed a spell of something which you get used to if you work for the BBC, which is a long period of not knowing where you are or what's happening, and waiting for someone, somewhere, to make a decision.

This went on until the beginning of 2023, at which point

we heard officially what some newspapers had been reporting for some time: that the show was cancelled. I was extremely upset about it, and so was Roy Clarke. Why were they doing this? No clear explanation was ever forthcoming. And OK, if six episodes was going to be too much of a stretch, what about just making three of the proposed six episodes – at least allowing the story to reach its conclusion? But no. All our protests and cajolings were to no avail. The moment had gone, apparently.

I had all sorts of reasons to regret and resent this decision. But in particular I regretted and resented it on behalf of Ronnie Barker. Does that sound odd? Let me explain.

I was fortunate enough to be able to call Ronnie B a friend, but, as you'll know if you've been with me in previous books (and paying attention), he was also a mentor. Very early on he spotted in me someone he could work with, and also someone he could help develop. Some of my earliest pieces of television were as part of the cast for the glorious bursts of madness which were Ronnie's late 1960s and early 1970s series, *Hark at Barker* and *His Lordship Entertains*.

And I was with him in *Porridge*, of course, the prison sitcom written by Dick Clement and Ian La Frenais, where I played Blanco opposite Ronnie's Norman Stanley Fletcher, arguably his greatest piece of comedy character creation. Being opposite Ronnie while he was bringing that character to life counts as one of the most electrifying experiences of my working life – and even a little bit eerie. The Ronnie you knew would entirely disappear and this person called Fletcher would be talking to you, with Ronnie nowhere in the room. I'd never seen a person so subsumed in the character he was playing.

He was eleven years my senior and well established, and he had long since worked out a lot of stuff that I was still struggling with at the time. He had such a mature perspective on it all and consequently, yes, he was someone from whom I learned all manner of things about comedy and playing roles and timing jokes and working with cameras and that sort of thing.

But even more than that, I watched the way he carried himself on a set and the way he interacted with others – always respectful, always willing to listen. I watched how, even though he was the star of the show, he made himself a team player, and the way that he always regarded the finished work as more important than his individual part in it.

Plus he had never lost touch with the fact that being paid to make people laugh is a rare privilege, never to be taken for granted. He was a role model all round, and I couldn't have asked for a better one.

'Working with Ron was easy,' Ronnie Corbett once said. 'He wrote a sketch and I queued for his lunch.'

Well, I, too, can vouch for Ronnie's interest in food. Breakfast might have been the most important meal of the day, but that didn't mean that lunch was in any way unimportant. And of course, there was no point downgrading the significance of supper, either. It was one of Ronnie B's mantras: 'You can't be funny on an empty stomach.'

But I can also vouch for the fact that working with Ronnie was easy.

Now, I had been around established actors before this. For example, I worked with Terry Scott on a couple of things. The first time was back in the sixties, when I was a nobody from repertory theatre who, to his own surprise, had come by his first, tiny television role – on the BBC's annual panto-mime. Terry was the star of that panto, and a big star in general, not just in British television but in British films as well. I was understandably quite mesmerised by him.

Soon after that, when my own star was burning no brighter, I got a small role in the sitcom Terry was starring in with Hugh Lloyd, *Hugh and I* – a small role, I might add, which got even smaller after Terry noticed that one of my lines was quite funny, had a quiet word with the director, and got the line switched to him. For this wet-behind-the-ears performer, who was still cautiously making his way into the business and in no position to complain, that was quite an eye-opening moment.

And then, in the 1980s, when I'd now made more of a name for myself, fate brought Terry and me back together again on *Danger Mouse*, where Terry played Danger Mouse's hamster sidekick, Penfold. (Code name 'the Jigsaw', of course, because at the first sight of trouble he fell to pieces.) Both of us were older and wiser by then, but Terry struck me as far more relaxed than I had remembered him from our initial encounters, and we got on very well during those sessions. No line-poaching – just a lot of laughter.

So, all in all, I think I'm well placed to say that Terry was a naturally talented comedian – perhaps as naturally talented as anyone I have worked with. He was an instinctively funny man.

But because it came instinctively to him, he was not a teacher – not someone who took other people along with him. He knew how it was done, and he didn't need or want to explain it to anyone else. He was in his own world – the world of his own talent. Many top-ranking comedians are like this.

Ronnie Barker was different. He, too, had an instinct for comedy, certainly, but he also had something which, in our business, is far rarer, which is an equal instinct for generosity. He really *was* a teacher. He could share what he knew, and he did so. And he could make space for the people around him to be funny, too.

I knew this very well from one particular experience with him on the first series of *Open All Hours*.

This was in 1976 – a time when Britain was hit by industrial turmoil, with strikes and unrest, plus soaring energy prices, a rising cost of living, political turmoil and constant arguments about our trading relationship with Europe.

Hard to imagine such a thing these days, isn't it?

Anyway, we'd reached the last episode of the first series,

and I found myself at a low ebb. This was nothing to do with the show itself. On the contrary, the filming had been going well, and I had been enjoying working with Ronnie enormously. The work was a pleasure, and so was the time off. There were those important meals, obviously. But on days off when we were on location in Yorkshire there were also the obligatory trips into the countryside so that Ronnie could hunt for bargains in the antique shops.

I'm not sure how useful I was to Ronnie on those trips. Basically, he would prowl round the shop, exercising his trained eye for a worthwhile piece while I followed somewhere behind him, picking up the odd thing and putting it down again and trying to look like I knew what I was doing.

But we had a lot of fun in the process – and maybe I even learned something about the value of unique ornamental pieces. Riding-boot lamps, for instance.

But there was this particular day during the filming when I was having a bad spell. Gloom had overcome me, and I was feeling despondent about where I was going with my career. Because, to me, at that point, it felt worryingly like nowhere.

Let's just briefly recap some of the false dawns I had endured to this point – the points where everything in my career seemed to be about to come up roses, only for the plant to wilt in the pot and all its leaves drop off.

First, the well-known one. Somewhere in 1968, I secured the part of Corporal Jones in a new sitcom by Jimmy Perry and David Croft called *Dad's Army* – only to unsecure it a matter of hours later when the BBC discovered that Clive Dunn (whom they had originally wanted for the role but thought they couldn't get) was available after all.

'Ah, well,' I had consoled myself. 'It was a long shot. Most likely nothing will come of that show anyway.'

And I then spent the ensuing eight years watching *Dad's Army* become one of the most popular comedies on television, on its way to embedding itself in the culture seemingly eternally.

Not to worry, though, because since then I'd got a job on *Do Not Adjust Your Set*, a zany children's sketch show attracting rave notices on ITV and all set to earn its cast secure employment and a lasting place in televisual history.

I have in my possession a letter from March 1968, typed on Rediffusion Television Limited headed notepaper, from Jeremy Isaacs – later Sir Jeremy, of course, and the former chief executive of Channel 4, but then producing some of Rediffusion's television output – and inviting me to lunch the following Wednesday.

Yes, a letter. It seems a little quaint now, possibly even as quaint as sending a messenger on horseback, but in those days, if you wanted to invite someone to lunch, you did so by post. And if you wanted to accept the invitation, you probably did that by post as well. I hate to say it, but the postal service was just that little bit more reliable back then. Try that today and the lunch would most likely be cold before you got there.

Anyway, Jeremy says further details will follow, but promises 'food, drink and talk about the future that lies ahead'. Oh, those heady days! Given the date, I can only assume that this was the meeting at which Jeremy confirmed plans for a second series of *Do Not Adjust Your Set*, and raised a glass to the future with me and the rest of the cast, namely Denise Coffey, Michael Palin, Terry Jones and Eric Idle.

When we made that second series, later that year, an American with long hair and an Afghan coat would come on board and begin supplying the show with cartoon sequences. That was Terry Gilliam.

You may already be spotting a connection between some of these people.

Yet only a year later, the last four of those mentioned would have ditched the programme and, without so much as a 'thanks and see you later', gone off to form a comedy troupe with a couple of other friends, called John Cleese and Graham Chapman, in order to make a madcap sketch show for adults.

And they had left yours truly and Denise behind, where our consolation prize from Rediffusion was to be given a children's show called *Two D's and a Dog*.

Have you ever seen *Two D's and a Dog*? I hope you haven't, in a way . . . It is not, shall we say, the most glittering of baubles on the decorated tree which is my career in show business. The D's of the title referred to the leading characters in this escapade: Dotty Charles, played by Denise, and

(CAUTION: terrible name for a character coming here – turn the page now if you are in any way sensitive to terrible puns which don't really take you anywhere) Dingle Bell, played by me.

And the dog in the title was an actual dog, played by an actual dog. An Old English sheepdog, to be precise, called Fido.

Maybe you've seen an Old English sheepdog in the commercials, doing clever things with Dulux paint pots or bounding attractively past freshly painted walls. Well, that was our dog, in one of his better paid and longer lasting roles.

OK, just to be exact, our Fido appeared in at least *some* of the Dulux ads. He wasn't in all of them. I hate to let light in on magic here, but I believe the Dulux dog changed from campaign to campaign. It was not always the same Dulux dog. But then (and apologies, again, if this is disturbing news to you), there were likewise a number of Rin-Tin-Tins, and a number of Lassies over the years. Such, I'm afraid, is the illusory nature of show business.

Anyhow, despite clearly being, at least to some extent, an experienced performer, I'm not sure acting was Fido's first love. Certainly it was quite hard to get him to sit still when you wanted him to sit still. And it was also quite hard to get him to move around when you wanted him to move around. And as for learning his cues . . .

Look, I'll say no more about Fido, in case his fan club comes after me. Or, even worse, his lawyer. But this was not

41

the happiest of shoots. I've been in shows that went out on the air and bombed. You have to accept that from time to time. But this was, I think, the only time I've been involved in a show where we all realised it was going to bomb even while we were filming it. I don't recommend being in that position. It tends to cause you to drag your feet a little on the way into work in the morning.

And meanwhile what were our former *Do Not Adjust Your Set* colleagues doing while Denise and I were trying to get a dog to sit up straight in a motorcycle sidecar? Well, don't worry about them unduly. For, yes, I think we can all agree that *Monty Python's Flying Circus*, much like *Dad's Army*, went on to do OK for itself.

Once again I seemed to have climbed on board a spaceship bound for the stratosphere, only to be asked to get out and go for sandwiches just before it launched.

One more item for this painful list of false starts: *The Top Secret Life of Edgar Briggs*, which went out on ITV in 1974. I got the lead in that series after auditions, and I couldn't have been more excited about it. At last, I thought: the solo comedy vehicle that will transform my fortunes!

Edgar Briggs is a member of the Secret Service who doesn't realise quite how bad he is at his job. Did someone mention Rowan Atkinson's Johnny English? There was certainly a foreshadowing of that in this show. But anyway, here was an opportunity to do lots of the physical comedy that I'd been honing in the theatre over the previous decade. The scripts had me diving onto sofas which then tipped over backwards, hanging out of windows, tumbling down staircases, and even plunging, fully clothed, into the Thames, which, given the current state of the water, would nowadays rank as the most physically reckless of these stunts.

Funnily enough, looking back, Briggs's flat in that series, with its orangey-brown curtains and its view of other flats through the window, was an awful lot like the Trotters' abode in Nelson Mandela House. Why, rough up the soft furnishings a bit and stick a sunburst wall-clock and a dopey plaster dog statue in there, and one could have passed almost exactly for the other.

Yet somehow that wasn't enough on its own to buy the series critical acclaim and a long life in the public's hearts. Indeed, the show came out a bit . . . well, the word 'raw' comes to mind. To be perfectly honest with you, I wince to think about it now. I was doing a lot of broad stuff that had worked really well for audiences in the theatre, but which I didn't have the experience to translate for the cameras, so it ended up looking overcooked, as if I was trying too hard – playing to the gallery, you could say, which was exactly what I *was* doing. Poor old Edgar bluffed and blustered his way through one series and was never asked back.

As the old theatrical saying has it: up like a rocket, down like a stick.

So, all this was behind me in 1976 while we were making that first series of *Open All Hours*. Not all that far up ahead of me, meanwhile, I could see my fortieth birthday looming, which felt pretty monumental. If I hadn't broken through by then, surely that was a signal that I never would – that my best opportunities had come and gone and all that lay ahead for me was a life of bit parts and playing second fiddle, just like I was in *Open All Hours* really.

Always the sidekick, I suppose you might say, and never the one doing the kicking.

Of course, now I can look back and shake my head and think: why was I so impatient? How lucky I was at that stage in my life to be working on a BBC sitcom with Ronnie Barker and laying some foundations to build on. But that's the calm wisdom of hindsight speaking, and clearly there was something restless inside me in those days that was agitating for more and worried that time and opportunity were not on my side.

When I went, glum-faced, to Ronnie and relayed these feelings to him, he urged me to be patient. But he did more than that. In order to cheer me up, he crafted a moment for Granville in the show.

It's there in that final episode of the series. We see Granville taking his heavily loaded delivery bike down a back alley and spotting, amid the piles of rubbish, a pair of bare legs poking straight up out of a bin. A concerned expression crosses his face. What on earth has he happened upon here?

On closer inspection, and to Granville's clear relief, these stray body parts turn out to be the detached limbs of a shop

mannequin. Granville inspects his find, and we sense a plan
hatching in his brain.

Cut to Granville cycling up the high street wearing a very
pleased-looking smile and with the legs sticking up merrily
out of the basket in front of him, the feet framing his ears
on each side.

We shot that during a busy morning in the middle of Doncaster. Those aren't extras turning and stepping off the pavement in startlement as Granville goes by; those are people
out shopping, doing genuine double takes at the sight.

Then cut again, to the park, and this time Granville is
seated on a bench, with his real legs folded beneath him and
his shirt untucked to form what at first glance could pass for
a white skirt, from beneath which the long bare plastic legs
extend outwards onto the path.

There he sits, half-man, half-mannequin. A rather
conventional-looking gentleman eating his lunch on a
bench opposite seems both confused and slightly threatened
by what he's seeing – even more so when Granville gives him
a coquettish look and crosses one of the legs over the other.
The gentleman gets up and hurries away.

And then Granville is back on his bike and on his way
again, and this time his attention is caught by the sight of
yet another pair of stray legs – this time protruding from
under a van, where the driver is evidently doing some repair
work. Again we watch an idea form in Granville's mind
before seeing him gleefully pedalling away, having (as we

subsequently learn when the camera pops back for a look) carefully laid the plastic legs on either side of the van driver's real ones, suggesting to anybody passing that there's more than just mechanics going on under that van.

The whole thing lasts just a bit more than a minute. It's an interlude, and in its little nod to silent comedy it has distant echoes, I guess, of one of the Captain Fantastic skits that I had done for *Do Not Adjust Your Set.* It certainly has nothing to do with the story the rest of the episode is telling. It's just a passage in which we see Granville, liberated from his stifling circumstances in the shop, and freed briefly from the over-bearing Arkwright, getting a moment to shine on his own.

How often in these shows we're acting out a version of something in our real lives.

And it's only there because Ronnie, in his generosity, sensed that I needed it and made it happen.

We were to make three more series of *Open All Hours* – but not immediately. There was a five-year gap between the first one, in 1976, and the second, in 1981. And really that only happened because the two Ronnies, Barker and Corbett, and their families had decided to spend a year living in Australia and the BBC suddenly had no new material from their prime comedy duo to bestow upon the nation. So some panicked scheduling executives rooted around in the cupboard and pulled out that first series of *Open All Hours* and sent it upstairs to be given another spin.

And that time it attracted far more attention than it had

the first time around, and new episodes were commissioned in time for Ronnie's return. So the show picked up from there, and even now, whenever people gather to make lists of the best British sitcoms, *Open All Hours* still tends to be part of the conversation, I'm proud to say.

Those rocky beginnings tend to get eclipsed by the show's subsequent success. Because the show came to mean something to people, it's hard to imagine there can have been a time when it was in danger of being overlooked. But in reality there are no foregone conclusions. A show can be as strong as you like in terms of its writing and its performances, but at some point it's going to come down to chance and timing and things you can't control or predict, not least the national mood.

It was the same with *Only Fools and Horses*, which had superb writing, courtesy of the late, great John Sullivan, and an ensemble cast with talent in depth that blended well and got on with each other superbly. Yet viewing figures for the first two series were only middling – approaching 7 million people.

True, nowadays that would be considered a blockbuster audience, the kind of numbers that big football matches generate. But back then, when there were only three channels to choose between and no such thing as the internet, it was the kind of underwhelming show of interest which had BBC executives pulling grim faces and reaching for the plug.

But then a gap opened up in the schedules, created by a

writers' strike, and, in the absence of new content, the BBC repeated those first two series and they did a little better.

And then that famous turning point occurred, when John Howard Davies, the BBC's head of comedy, sat at his desk with the scripts for series three in a pile on one side of him, and the viewing figures on a sheet of paper on the other side of him and declared that his head was with the viewing figures but his gut was with the scripts. And then, in a decision which caused all of us to cheer John Howard Davies's gut to the rafters, he decided to back the scripts and green-lit series three.

On such perilous acts of whim in a person's office does the entire future of comedy tremble. John Howard Davies didn't live to regret his instinct, and neither did the rest of us. The viewing figures for series four of *Only Fools* were double those of series one and the show was finally on its way, heading for regular week-night audiences of 16 million and for Christmas specials whose viewing figures would shred records and rival the crowds typically drawn by moon landings and cup finals.

I recently dug out of a drawer an old newspaper clipping which has obviously been knocking about in my office since February 1994 – or so my scrawl in biro down one side of it tells me. I don't keep very many cuttings. But I have kept this one.

Culled from the *Daily Telegraph*, the piece is a review of the latest television viewing figures, and it's headlined 'JASON

AND THE ADDED NOUGHTS'. (Argonauts . . . added noughts . . . you will see what they did there, I am sure.)

The gist of the story is that the BBC has recently recovered its audience share to 44 per cent – its best numbers in quite a while. But as the article points out, there is no room for complacency on the Beeb's part. 'The platform for this recovery is narrow,' it states, 'a repeat of the 1990 *Only Fools and Horses* special having delivered 12.27 million viewers on the Sunday.'

Let's just pause a moment to ponder that number. More than 12 million viewers for a repeat showing of a four-year-old comedy show! It was remarkable then, and it would be impossible now.

However, the point of the report is that ITV are by no means out of the running here. The piece highlights the 10 million viewers generated for the commercial broadcaster by a murder drama called *Dandelion Dead* – an audience which is not to be sneezed at, if I may use that expression in the context of dandelions.

But that audience is still reported as being 'in stark contrast to the 15 million-plus' that a certain ITV detective show had been attracting around that time, and no doubt would again very soon.

'Given the recent performance of *A Touch of Frost*,' the report concludes, 'the bankability of David Jason has never been more obvious.'

Dear reader, what can I tell you? Naturally, modesty insists that I blush fetchingly to see my bankability so resoundingly trumpeted in the national press.

But blimey, if you had shown that newspaper clipping to the actor who, eighteen years earlier, had confessed to Ronnie Barker that he was feeling thwarted and getting nowhere and wondering about junking it all . . . well, clearly that actor would have accused you of winding him up in the most heartless possible fashion.

And if those little bits of happenstance hadn't occurred to keep *Open All Hours* and *Only Fools* alive when the odds were stacked against them, then who knows how differently it might all have ended up? People knock repeats on television, but you won't find me saying a word against them. Indeed, I don't know where I would be without them.

We lost Ronnie Barker in 2005, and there were two thousand people at his memorial service which took place five months later in the grandeur of Westminster Abbey, no less. As you'll be aware, it's mostly royalty that gets the come-on-down for a big service at the Abbey. Only two other comedians had been commemorated in that nationally important building before Ronnie: Joyce Grenfell and Les Dawson. Such was Ronnie's public standing at the end of his life.

I was there, and so was Nick Lyndhurst. So were Lynda Baron, Bernard Cribbins, June Whitfield, Michael Palin (my old comrade from *Do Not Adjust Your Set*), Richard Briers, Tim Brooke-Taylor, Ben Elton . . . just a never-ending parade, it seemed, of friends and admirers, many of them key players in British television comedy.

So it was never likely to be a strictly serious occasion, even given the surroundings. There was, of course, a procession of four candles, alluding to the famous *Two Ronnies* hardware shop sketch. But I mostly recall Ronnie Corbett, in his eulogy, telling the story of how Ronnie, a fiercely private man, had sought reassurance that the clinic he was attending for his heart trouble was a place of the utmost discretion and unlikely to leak the story.

The person at the clinic told him it most certainly was a discreet place – watertight, indeed. And then he added, in a confiding tone, 'We had that Danny La Rue in the other week.'

Peter Kay spoke, too. He had once written Ronnie a fan letter – and then got a reply on HMP Slade-headed notepaper, written entirely in the voice of Fletch, Ronnie's character in *Porridge*. Kay replied by sending him a nail file. That had started a long correspondence, and the respect between the pair of them was mutual.

There was no time, alas, to tell one of my favourite Ronnie B stories which revolved around the time the great comedy writer Barry Cryer tried to trick Ronnie at a book signing. Cryer went along in disguise, in sunglasses, with his collar turned up and a hat pulled down, and queued with everyone else to get his book signed.

When he reached the front of the line, he put on an

American accent and asked Ronnie to sign the book to John Smith. Ronnie duly wrote in the book, closed it and pushed it across the table to him.

Cryer left in triumph, having successfully deceived Ronnie B, and was looking forward to telling him about it later.

At home he opened the book. On the title page, Ronnie had written, 'P--- off, Cryer, can't you see I'm busy?'

The sermon at the memorial service was delivered by Ronnie himself – a recording of the sketch he did for *The Two Ronnies* as a vicar who realises a party of cockneys is in the congregation for evensong and targets his address accordingly by delivering it in rhyming slang.

And so the magnificent architecture of the Abbey reverberated to Ronnie sonorously enunciating the parable of the man whose trouble and strife has run off with a tea leaf and who thus finds himself living with his eldest bricks and mortar, but is short of bees and honey, so is struggling to pay the Burton-on-Trent . . .*

---

* Just in case a glossary might be of service: trouble and strife = wife, tea leaf = thief, bricks and mortar = daughter, bees and honey = money, Burton-on-Trent = rent. Later in the sermon, the man in the tale spots, on the pavement in front of him, 'a small, brown Richard the Third', but I'll leave you to decode that one. (Clue: it's not what you first think. Indeed, as the sermon unfolds, the man selflessly decides to remove the small, brown Richard the Third from the pavement before anyone treads on it. To this end, he reaches down and gently picks it up. Then he holds the small, brown Richard the Third in the palm of his hand. And the small, brown Richard the Third flies away.)

It was an amazing occasion – warm and funny and slightly surreal, as Ronnie would have wished it to be, and I think it all helped us come to terms a bit more with what we had lost. I would say that's the gift of occasions like those, and the most you can hope for from them.

But I think my own personal attempt to find some lasting closure about Ronnie's death came later, and it took the form of *Still Open All Hours*.

It put me back in the same shop on the same street in Doncaster – a hairdressing establishment normally, but still happy to let us move in for a few weeks and stand all the old items out on the street. A few years earlier the place had been in danger of demolition in a proposed purge of ageing housing stock by the council. I was grateful they changed their minds and that it was still standing. It's only the exterior shots, of course, and we could have recreated the shop somewhere else easily enough. But it wouldn't have been the same.

I liked having that solid connection between the two shows. I liked that Granville was standing in the same doorway, looking up the same street. I liked the sense that so much had changed in the forty years that had passed since the first series, and yet that nothing had changed, because that seemed to me to be very true about life in general.

So that's what eats me a bit about the cancellation of the show right at the end, when the finish line was in sight. The failure to complete and tie up a story when we were all set to do so would have been frustrating in the context of any show. I would have felt it about *A Touch of Frost* after fifteen series, and about *The Darling Buds of May* after two.

But it was especially so for me here. I always saw *Still Open* as a tribute to Ronnie, a way of thanking him for all that he had done for me. I was completing the circle, in a way, and so not being able to bring those strings together at the end and finish the job tidily left me feeling sad.

Still, at least Ronnie's presence was there in the shows that we did make. It was there in the shop's cash register – that lethal finger-trap that seemed to have vengeance in its heart for anyone who dared operate it. I couldn't go near that fickle cash drawer without seeing Ronnie's Arkwright, jumping back as it slammed, and flexing his shoulders and then somehow brilliantly catching whatever had just been dislodged from the top of it.

We had Arkwright's presumed ghost causing the lights to flicker on and off a couple of times, as if in stark commentary on Granville's behaviour. And then there were the scenes in which Granville is in conversation with the framed photograph of Arkwright that hung at the back of the shop. Those were some of my favourite moments in the script – though quite difficult to do without choking up sometimes.

But really it's no different in my life. Ronnie feels constantly present to me there, as well. So when I spoke to the portrait in those shows, in many ways I was just acting out a conversation which takes place in my mind all the time.

Like I say to the picture at one point: 'Eee, you taught me some stuff, didn't you, eh?'

I have a little fantasy in which, at some point in the future, beset by a writers' strike, or maybe a train strike, or whatever kind of strike happens to be available at the time, the BBC finds itself re-screening all the old series of *Still Open All Hours* to fill a hole in the schedules.

And then, in the face of booming viewing figures and brightly glowing notices, they are forced to bring the show back and commission those final clinching episodes. And I finally get to bring the curtain down on the story and close up the old shop properly for the last time.

Unlikely? Well, perhaps. But you can't say it hasn't happened with programmes I've been in before.

This time in a couple of years . . .

CHAPTER TWO

Of quiz shows, Wombles and voices on the radio

At some point in the days after the cancellation of *Still Open All Hours*, I was idly rooting around in a drawer in my office, having nothing much else to do, when, under some crumpled pieces of paper and a file of notes, I turned up an old diary. Indeed, more than four decades old.

You'll be picturing the scene, no doubt, as my trembling hands withdrew this forgotten volume from the obscurity of its hiding place. Old diaries! Is there anything more poignant? Is there anything more likely to whisk us through history's beaded curtain and into the walk-in larder where our former selves are ever-lingering?

You'll be imagining me, then, setting a weighty volume down on the desk and, in a trance of wonderment, using my fingertips to clear the dust from its leather cover, exposing the gold-embossed lettering below. And you'll be imagining the eager and yet somehow anxious expression on my face as I anticipated the deluge of my innermost thoughts and

57

feelings that doubtless awaited me in this treasure trove's closely inked pages.

Well, not quite. It was hardly dusty at all, in fact, and it was the *Sunday Telegraph* 'slimline' Gardener's Diary for 1979.

You'll mock, I know – especially in these days of calendar apps, synced to all your devices. But, look, this was the 1970s – a whole other era for personal organisation. We're even some years pre-Filofax at this point, and many more pre-iPhone. If you had said to me in 1979, as I made haste to make note on these narrow pages of yet another key meeting with a top-flight television commissioning executive (ahem), 'One day you'll have all that information on your phone, you know,' I would have been obliged to reply, 'But how's that going to work? The phone's plugged into the wall.'

Yes, this is what we had in those all-but-forgotten times before Wi-Fi. We had the *Sunday Telegraph* 'slimline' Gardener's Diary, in a handy pocket- or handbag-friendly format. And into the *Sunday Telegraph* Gardener's Diary we entered, in our own handwriting, using our own biro, all the appointments of our hectic working lives so that we wouldn't forget them.

Or I clearly did, anyway.

Nevertheless, a gardener's diary . . . why was it this diary in particular that I came to be using? It puzzles me. Because I don't need to point out that other diaries would have been available. Archaeologists' diaries, church bell-ringers' diaries, hamster-breeders' diaries . . . possibly even actors' diaries. I could have had my pick, presumably.

You see, the thing is, being a gardener's diary, this pocket-book includes, both before and after the actual diary section, many pages relating to matters horticultural – reminders about when you should be planting out your seedlings, composting your beds, pruning your rambler roses, etc. And it also supplies an extensive list of the country's garden centres for when you need one in a hurry, which, as a gardener, you almost always do.

All useful information, of course – but much more useful, I'm bound to submit, if you actually had a garden. And in this particular phase of my life, I didn't. Not unless you count the windowsill overlooking the courtyard outside the kitchen of my upper-floor flat in Newman Street.

That was the ledge on which I periodically stood the solitary item of greenery in my life – a potted grapefruit plant – so that it could enjoy the unrivalled view of the brick wall opposite and take restorative gulps of the delicious and invigorating central London air.

Which didn't do it any harm, by the way. As I have already recalled in gripping detail in an earlier volume of these memoirs, that grapefruit plant – tenderly raised by my own green fingers from the grapefruit pip which nearly killed me when I choked on it over breakfast one morning – thrived and thrived.

Travelling on with me when I eventually moved away to

Sussex and then to Buckinghamshire, that grapefruit plant duly became a bush and then something closer to a tree. And in that latter form it currently spends the warmer months nodding gently to itself in a large earthenware pot at my present abode, where I *do* have a garden, and where that carefully nurtured grapefruit plant provides sweet daily proof of the old adage that what doesn't kill you grows into something nice and leafy for the shrubbery.*

Still, tending that plant in a far smaller form was the only kind of gardening that I was up to in 1979, so all the advice in this specialist's diary was a bit surplus to requirements. Indeed, the news that January would be an optimum time for me to be 'protecting tender perennials by covering the crowns with weathered ashes, straw or bracken' would have meant very little to me and to most other readers dwelling just north of Oxford Street at that moment, where bracken tended to be in quite short supply.

As for 'tender perennials', I suppose they weren't entirely unheard of round my way. But there was a pharmacist nearby for that kind of emergency who seemed to know what he was talking about, so I'd say we were pretty well covered in that direction.

And as for the 'Draft Calendar of Shows and Competitions'

* The grapefruit continues to do well, thank you for asking. No further attempts to fruit since I last wrote about it, but obviously I will keep you informed and let you know the moment anything sprouts.

scheduled for 1979 by the Royal Horticultural Society . . . well, short of me deciding to enter in the home-cured grapefruit category, those pages of the diary were of no more relevance to me at the time than . . . well, the postal address of the Scottish National Sweet Pea, Rose & Carnation Society in Motherwell that the diary also thoughtfully supplied.

So why was the *Sunday Telegraph* Gardener's Diary my constant companion throughout 1979? Did it come free with the newspaper one weekend? Perhaps. Did you have to save up tokens and send off for it? More likely. But I didn't even *read* the *Sunday Telegraph*, let alone cut bits out of it and set them aside every week.

Was it a Christmas gift, then? Had it been lovingly wrapped and labelled and handed to me with a warm smile during the festivities of 1978? Quite possibly. And had the person who gifted it got it free with the newspaper, perhaps by sending off tokens? Also possible.

Bloomin' cheapskate!

But wherever it came from, this diary certainly saw some heavy use. Why, its week-to-a-page spreads are positively crammed with scrawls and jottings in my fair hand. In fact, as I first cast my eye over its stuffed pages, it caused me a moment or two of rueful reflection, I don't mind admitting. The contrast with my post-lockdown predicament couldn't have been sharper. These heavily biro-scored pages, bursting with demands upon my time, seemed, at that particular juncture, almost to be mocking me.

What the pages *don't* contain, it's true, is much in the way of my innermost thoughts and feelings, which, as alluded to earlier, is something you might reasonably be looking for from an old diary. But that's hardly surprising. Look at all those appointments! What time would there have been for deeper reflections? I was far too busy keeping a diary to keep a diary. And busy is really only the half of it. I was basically – as we say in the world of elite equestrianism – trying to ride three horses with one backside.

So let's allow these pages to fall open at random, shall we? Let's see that overburdened backside in action. And let's seek in this ancient document some insights into the working life of a 39-year-old actor on the cusp of something, though he doesn't yet have the faintest idea what.

Sunday 18 February, Rehearsal, Blankety Blank, 3.30, BBC TV Studios.

Now, this will come as a huge shock to you, I'm sure.

No, not the fact that in 1979, ahead of nearly all of the television work which would make my name, my reputation was already starry enough to put me on a game-show platform with the likes of Wendy Craig, Larry Grayson and Barbara Windsor – though I admit that is slightly surprising.

No, the big shock here, surely, is that *Blankety Blank* was something for which there was a *rehearsal*.

It so rarely looked like it. The general atmosphere of the *Blankety Blank* game show was of things slowly and gently falling apart, not least the prizes – the unimpressive crystal glasses, the glum-looking saucepan sets. Les Dawson, who hosted the show after Terry Wogan, used to refer to the gifts the contestants went home with as 'fire-salvaged'.

Plus, of course, there was the show's fabled consolation trophy – the 'silver' *Blankety Blank* chequebook and pen.

The significance of that trophy rather dies in the air, of course, in this cashless age, when nobody writes any kind of cheque any more, let alone a blank one. But the key thing here, from a social history point of view, is that those *Blankety Blank* trophies were ornaments of really quite astonishing cheapness, to which I can attest, having seen one up close.

Or as Dawson used to tell the contestants: 'You'll never be short of something to prop your door open with now.'

I seem to have gone on *Blankety Blank* a couple of times in this year, and I have no doubt that I felt quite flattered to be invited. I probably felt it was going to boost my standing in some way, too, though that may have been a naive hope. But I certainly remember getting a decent line away about the ridiculous novelty microphone that Terry Wogan was obliged to roam around with – a long, thin silver wand, a bit like an old car aerial, with a little globe at the tip of it.

'Twenty of these shows, and you still haven't finished that toffee apple, have you?'

Not bad. However, my mockery of that daft contraption was soon to be put entirely in the shade by Kenny Everett, a loose cannon at the best of times, who, just a couple of weeks later, plucked the microphone from Wogan's hands and calmly bent it through ninety degrees before handing it back to him.

In comedy as in life, actions speak louder than words.

I knew Terry a little – not well, but I don't think there were many people who would claim to have known him well. Terry seemed very good at holding the world at arm's length – a bit like Ronnie B in that regard. And he must have felt he really needed to at times, because he was the biggest broadcaster in Britain in that period and his fame was enormous – the kind of fame that could eat you whole if you weren't very careful with it.

But I admired him enormously and we had some fun together. I knew off by heart the Sir Henry Newbolt poem, 'Vitaï Lampada', or 'The Torch of Life' – the Victorian verse that begins 'There's a breathless hush in the Close tonight' and includes the line 'Play up! play up! and play the game!' Terry loved that poem and he would get me to recite it almost every time I bumped into him. I ended up going on his Radio 2 show and reciting it there as well. He stopped short of asking me to recite it on *Blankety Blank*, though.

I don't suppose it occurred to either of us back then, bantering over a stupid microphone, that our names would eventually appear, nominated for knighthoods, on the same Queen's Birthday Honours List, in 2005. But it came to pass. In later years, Terry would say about me to other people:

'He owes it all to me for granting him the opportunity to be funny on *Blankety Blank*.' Well, it's a theory.

But there's another equally compelling argument that I risked everything I had, professionally speaking, by accepting the opportunity to be funny on *Blankety Blank*. And that somehow I got away with it.

Those seventies episodes of *Blankety Blank* will look gloriously naff today – although the show is still with us, I believe, so it must have been doing something right. And in some ways, I guess, it was ahead of its time. There was that great sea change in television quiz shows in the 1990s when they all went a bit postmodern, if I may use the term. That was the moment when quizzes stopped being about people trying to get the answers to the questions right, and started being about people deliberately getting the answers to the questions wrong for a laugh, and only then trying to get them right.

The *Have I Got News for You* approach, you might call it. And you could argue that *Blankety Blank*, in its own sweet and rambling way, opened the door for all of that. Certainly there had been few quiz shows before that on which people spent quite so much time getting things wrong.

And there had been no quiz shows on which the hosts were encouraged to be so scathing about the quality of the show itself – so wantonly unenthusiastic from the off. *Blankety Blank* was the anti-game show before anti-game shows were invented. Maybe I can be proud to have been part of its history.

Which might not be quite the case with the following . . .
Wednesday 25 April, Celebrity Squares? Evening.

Blimey, I was hot on the prime-time game-show circuit in 1979, wasn't I? On a veritable streak! Ignore the question mark in this diary entry: it happened. I did my turn on ITV's *Celebrity Squares* – one of nine 'celebrities' sitting in rows of three in a set of hutches designed to resemble a noughts and crosses chart.

You had to answer the guests' questions for them. If you got it right, they could put a nought or a cross in your square and try and complete a line. Maybe you remember. Either way, you get the idea.

Bob Monkhouse was the presenter. I knew Bob well. I'd done parts in his radio show *Mostly Monkhouse* in the early seventies, and we'd done summer seasons together, appeared in farces in Weston-super-Mare, among other places with end-of-the-pier theatres, where I had learned two things.

Firstly, that Bob Monkhouse was one of the most formidable controllers of an audience that I had ever witnessed. There wasn't a person in a packed auditorium that he couldn't reach and involve.

Secondly, that there was nobody more dedicated than Bob to the noble and ancient craft of causing his fellow actors to corpse. Quite simply nobody, surely, has gone to such lengths to put his colleagues off, mid-show.

And I don't just mean stripping stark naked in the wings where I could catch sight of him in all his glory – though he did do that. I mean practically booby-trapping the stage with items designed to throw your concentration through a loop.

One play we were in made great use of a basket supposedly containing a baby, the role of which was played in the usual course of things by a doll, tucked mostly out of sight of the audience. But the doll very soon stopped appearing in that basket, Bob having replaced it with . . . well, I tremble to recall the things I saw, peering into that receptacle over the course of that summer. I'll just mention the sausages. And my underwear, snatched by Bob one night in a raid on my dressing room. There were other far less wholesome things, trust me.

Bob had an idea at one point that he wanted to develop a silent movie, which would pay tribute to the greats of the era. He talked to me about helping him with it, because that was one of my enthusiasms too. I can remember having discussions with him about it as we walked around his very lovely garden. (The grounds of Bob's house were superb. Now, there was someone who could genuinely have used a copy of the *Sunday Telegraph* Gardener's Diary.) Sadly nothing came of it, which was a pity. I think it would have been good.

So was all of this why I got the come-on-down for *Celebrity Squares*? It may have been. Either way, I remember thinking the set was a bit crudely knocked together. The steps that took you up to the perches on the upper floors were rather thin and haphazard – like window cleaners' ladders. It was – the former electrician in me couldn't help but notice – a bit like being back on a building site. If there had been a bucket of plaster and a couple of hods of bricks lying about, the illusion would have been complete.

Still, again, it was very flattering in a way to find yourself sitting up there on that platform – an endorsement of sorts, proof that you had not gone entirely unnoticed. And in 1979, in my late thirties, flying around madly and still trying to figure out where I fitted in, I was clearly grateful for any sense of inclusion I could find.

* * *

I would quickly work out that this kind of TV exposure, as alluring as it was, was something that I needed to be careful with. There were risks attached. Let me put it this way: the more you did this kind of thing, the more this became the kind of thing you did. There were people (no names, no pack drill) who you saw on these shows, who eventually you *only* saw on these shows. And, fun though it might be every now and again, it wasn't what I wanted. The plan I had was to find some space for myself as an actor encompassing the whole range of what the word actor meant, if I possibly could. The plan wasn't appearances as a celebrity on game shows, no matter how gifted the host.

Even at the time I don't think I felt entirely comfortable up there on that noughts and crosses frame with the likes of Willie Rushton and Isla St Clair – and it wasn't *completely* to do with the rickety set. I already knew that I was only really at ease in front of audiences if I had a character to hide behind, an invented person that I could disappear into.

'Just be yourself,' producers would say, as if nothing could be simpler. But I didn't really have what you needed for that. I was too self-conscious, and not relaxed enough in my own skin, the way you have to be. Quite shy, frankly. Which might sound a bit odd coming from an actor. But actually a lot of actors are shy. It's why we become actors. Acting can get you around many of your problems with shyness very efficiently.

People would be expecting laughs, too, but being funny off the cuff is its own art, and it was never really mine. I was a comic actor, but that is a very different thing from being a comic. Comics are a breed unto themselves.

And that was something I had known with painful clarity ever since my debut performance as a stand-up comedian – my debut performance as a stand-up comedian which, for reasons which will shortly become apparent, was also my final performance as a stand-up comedian.

This little adventure was all Malcolm Taylor's fault. It was Malcolm who had offered me a role in a London production of Dylan Thomas's *Under Milk Wood* that he was directing. That was one of my earliest professional breaks and the start of a long and firm friendship between us. But we were both merely scratching a living in those days, and during a particularly flat period for business, Malcolm, who fancied himself as a bit of an entrepreneur, asked me if I had ever thought about giving stand-up a go.

'You know some jokes,' Malcolm said. 'You like joking around, making people laugh.'

There was, he felt, a niche for me there. And maybe a niche for him as my manager.

I wasn't so sure. It was true that I did love telling jokes and stories and hearing people laugh. But even while fully a-flame with the ambition of youth, I was aware that there was a large step between cracking a gag to get a snigger out of your pals and having the London Palladium in the palm of your hand.

Malcolm could be very persuasive, though. Maybe stand-up *was* a direction I could go in. And it wasn't like I had much else happening for me at that point.

I heard myself saying, 'All right, I'll give it a shot.'

This was over a decade earlier than my gardener's diary days, back in the mid-1960s. Near Malcolm's house in Maida Vale was a pub that did amateur comedy nights. You might not know the pub, but you'll know, I feel sure, the scene: a microphone in a corner, and a largely uninterested audience of locals, many of whom have come in for a drink with their friends and aren't automatically going to be happy when somebody suddenly interrupts their conversation with five minutes of material that they haven't asked for.

It never feels promising.

Still, Malcolm went in one day and charmed the landlord,

telling him he had this young guy, born comic, trying to get on, bound to go down well . . . And the next thing I knew I had a gig in the diary as a stand-up.

I can't remember what fee Malcolm negotiated for my prospective comic services – or if there even *was* a fee. A fiver, maybe? Or I may have been paid solely in leftover sandwiches from the previous night's darts match. But no matter either way. This was all about the future. Like everything, really, in those days.

As for my act . . . well, I wrote out some jokes I knew. And I went to Malcolm's flat and worked with him on my delivery. We took it quite seriously.

To be honest, I can't remember exactly which prized jewels from my extensive personal repertoire of zingers made it into the act. But if you think of jokes along the lines of 'My wife's just been abroad/Jamaica?/ No, she went of her own accord', you'll be in the right area.

Is it possible that I went on that night and told the audience about the man whose dog had no nose? And about the person who asked that man how, in that case, his dog smelt? And how the man replied 'Terrible'?

Reader, it's not just possible – it's highly likely.

So on I went, and what can I say? It was an absolute disaster. Looking back, this was where I truly learned the theatrical meaning of dying a death. Right there in that quarter-full pub, beyond any wince-inducing audition, beyond any limp piece of business in an under-cooked farce on some pier

71

somewhere . . . that was where I knew what it felt like to want the floor to swallow you whole and for time to reverse and for everyone to wake up and not remember anything about what had just happened.

I can still recall it – the sensation of standing there with that microphone and losing control of the room, feeling the audience's attention wander away from me and realising that I had no hope at all of getting it back again. It was desperate. I thought I was physically shrinking. I was getting smaller and smaller with every second that passed.

And this was especially worrying because I wasn't that tall to begin with.*

And, lord, the speed with which I was babbling! Ten minutes of material, Malcolm had promised the landlord, and ten minutes of material was what we had prepared in Malcolm's flat. But that was without an increasingly uninterested audience in front of me, and a sense of panic surging through me and causing me to push the accelerator down.

Timing – famously the secret of great comedy – went straight out the pub's front window and instead I found myself involuntarily trying to achieve some kind of land-speed record for words per minute. I must have rattled off that material in well under five minutes. Indeed, dear reader, it's possible that, at that very moment, I invented rap, at

---

* I am five foot six, on a good day, fully extended. But so is Oprah Winfrey, and it hasn't held *her* back.

least two decades before anyone else had the idea. And fat lot of credit I get for it.

And then I left the stage to the sound of one person clapping, which was almost certainly Malcolm.

And this is why, even now, whenever I'm asked if I would be happy to 'make an appearance' somewhere, I'm always gripped by the fear that I will be likely to . . . well, make an absolute appearance of myself.

Blame that pub in Maida Vale.

But let us draw a curtain and move on – as that pub audience only wished it could have done. And let us cleave once more to the gardener's diary in 1979.

Thursday 6 September, Molinare, 2 o'clock, Redy Brek.

OK, so this is me heading off to the Molinare recording studio not far from Carnaby Street, there to lend my dulcet tones (or whatever tones the client's brief requires) to an advertisement for Ready Brek, the famously warming oat-based cereal with which I am sure you are familiar.

Perhaps you also recall how, according to seventies legend, a serving of this formidable breakfast comestible would cast around its consumer a protective orange glow, not unlike radioactivity in cartoon books, yet fit to see off the coldest morning. And no doubt the comfortingly fruity tone of my voice, intoning the legendary pay-off, 'Ready Brek – central heating for kids', was intended to cause a similar effect in the listener.

By the way, forgive the misspelling of the client's name

in the above diary entry, which I should, of course, have recorded as 'Ready Brek'. My mistake. But if you're going with 'Brek' in your brand name, you're inviting people to get 'Redy' in their heads, aren't you?

Still, porridge: that's a good, wholesome product, no matter how you spell it. The kind of product anyone would be proud to get behind. I was doing the country a service there.

But wait, because there's also this, from earlier in the year: *Thursday 21 June, Molinare, 3 o'clock, Silk Cut.*

So, just to decode: what was on the cards here was a mid-afternoon trip to the same Molinare recording facility, but this time to speak up on behalf of what was possibly, at that point, the country's most popular brand of low-tar cigarettes.

And there you have the life of the active voice artist in a nutshell. One day you were pointing the nation the way of a healthy breakfast, the next you were offering it a fag. I don't know what to say to you about that, except that it was all work.

And, good grief, there were a lot of these commercial voice-over engagements out there for me in 1979 – a real flurry of them, page after page in the diary. This would have been the period when the agency I was signed up with for voice work issued me with a pager to clip to my belt so that they could reach me wherever I happened to be. The only other people I knew who had pagers in those days were hospital doctors on call. But clearly it was possible also to be a voice artist on call, and whenever a job came up my pager would buzz and I would hurry away importantly to find a phone and call Linda at the agency, who would tell me where I needed to be.

Think of me in that moment, if you will, as the voice-over world's equivalent of Superman. Kind of Voiceoverman.

'They're in trouble with a radio commercial for throat lozenges over in Wardour Street, and if it's not done by three, there'll be hell to pay! Can you help us, Voiceoverman?'

'Tell them I'm on my way and to do nothing until I get there!'

Now, I knew actors who thought this kind of work was beneath them – that, frankly, it wasn't what proper actors were meant to be doing with their days. But I certainly didn't think that. Would I have rather been sitting at home, keeping my powder dry and waiting for the big, career-changing role to come up, or bolting around Soho advocating on behalf of porridge or cigarettes or whichever product seemed to need me? The latter definitely, because the latter meant I was working.

Also, if it was good enough for Sir Michael Hordern . . .

I've told before, many times, my story about bumping into Sir Michael one afternoon at one of the sound studios – possibly Molinare, actually – and not being able to suppress my surprise at seeing one of the true greats of the theatre in this slightly . . . well, *grubby* context.

I mean, if we're talking about proper actors, you can't get much more proper than Sir Michael Hordern, can you?

'What are *you* doing here, Sir Michael?' I heard my shocked self ask as we encountered each other in the reception area.

'Why, dear boy, the same as you,' came Sir Michael's reply. 'Being a vocal *whore*.'

And, look: I've just gone and told that story again! But I know why I love repeating it: it's because every time I do so I get to do my impression of *the voice* – Michael's wonderfully rich and tremulous tone in which the word 'whore' grows at least one other syllable and becomes 'hu-werrr'.

Once a voice artist, always a voice artist.

Anyway, 'hu-werr' or otherwise, I've never had cause to regret the time I spent in those voice studios. It was all good grounding, and, in a roundabout way, those experiences would eventually lead me to some of the character work that I'm proudest of – not just *Danger Mouse*, which I've already mentioned, but also giving voice to Toad in the Cosgrove Hall animation of Kenneth Grahame's *The Wind in the Willows*, and to the character of the giant in *The BFG* from the Roald Dahl book, which Cosgrove Hall also animated.

In fact, thinking about it, by 1979 I must have already occupied a position of quite some good standing in the voice-lending community, because by then I had already been a Womble.

Yes, a Womble. Oh, what it was, in the mid-1970s, to be able to claim a connection with the furry, long-nosed litter-pickers of Wimbledon Common. At that point in our nation's history the Wombles were everywhere – even more so than litter, frankly. They were stars of Elizabeth Beresford's children's books, stars of the small screen – pop stars, even, thanks to Mike Batt and his extremely catchy music.

And in 1977 they became film stars, too – granted their own full-length, live-action movie with nationwide cinema release. And I joined them on that journey to wide-screen immortality by providing what the movie's credits, as they slide up the screen at the end there, would formally denote as 'Womble Voices'.

At this point, after a pause in which a confused and worried look has crossed your face, I hear your anxious and slightly quailing voice ask: 'But, David . . . if the Wombles were in the movie, why didn't they just use their *own* voices?'

Which query is, of course, my cue to pull myself up short, smile reassuringly and hastily add: 'Ah, well, now, I'm sure the Wombles would have supplied their own voices if they had been in a position to. But I expect they were just far too busy that day picking up litter and ensuring that our world is a tidier and a better place. You know what those Wombles are like! Oh, and also they were played in the movie by blokes in giant furry costumes who, understandably, would have a job speaking from inside all that fur. So they needed to get an actor in to put the voices on afterwards.'

I hope I'm not ruining anybody's cherished illusions here.

77

So yes, I dubbed a Womble on the movie *Wombling Free*.*
Actually, I think I may have dubbed more than one Womble:
don't hold me to it, but perhaps I did Wellington as well as
Orinoco. Might I also have done Tomsk? It's not beyond the
bounds of possibility. There were certainly more Wombles to
go round than voices in the studio to play them, as I recall,
so I think we all did a bit of doubling up.

However – proud? Reader, proud doesn't even *begin* to
cover my feelings in the wake of that commission. To be on
board the mighty Womble-branding juggernaut as it swept
across Britain in the mid-1970s, even as the smallest cog in
its rumbling engine, was to be at the beating heart of the
national culture at that moment in history. It was an absolute honour.

And I think the money was quite decent, too.

It certainly *should* have been decent, because this was a
major production – definitely the spiffiest film production
I had been involved in up to that point. It was directed by
Lionel Jeffries who had made the wonderful and still hugely
revered *The Railway Children*. It featured among its cast the
superb Frances de la Tour and David Tomlinson, who, you
may well know, was no slouch in the family film department,
having been in *Mary Poppins* and *Bedknobs and Broomsticks*,

---

* Interestingly, the software on this computer seems to want to autocor-
rect *Wombling Free* to *Wobbling Free*. But that's a different kind of movie
altogether, surely.

not to mention *The Love Bug*, an exquisite car-based movie to rank with the best of them, in my humble opinion.*

And it featured Bonnie Langford, who was only thirteen at the time, but had already been a star for the best part of seven years, which is what you call getting your career off to a properly early start.†

My fellow Womble-voicers were pretty top-drawer as well. They included Jon Pertwee, who had recently spent four years as Doctor Who, and Janet Brown, the tremendously funny comedian who could do a fantastic impression of the woman who had just become the new leader of the Conservative Party – a certain Margaret Thatcher.‡

So if the quiz question 'What connects Britain's first woman prime minister with Madame Cholet of the Wombles?' ever comes up, you will now have your answer handy, if you didn't already.

---

* The car in question was a Volkswagen Beetle. If you ask me, no automobile in action-film history has appeared to be quite so fully possessed of a character. And yes, I'm including *Chitty Chitty Bang Bang* in the reckoning here. Argue with me if you wish, but I'm right.

† Bonnie Langford really was only six years old when she came to public attention by winning the talent show *Opportunity Knocks*. I don't just make this stuff up, you know. There's some proper research going on here. Incidentally, I'm not sure what I was up to at the age of six but I'm absolutely sure it wasn't impressing Hughie Greene with a song and a dance.

‡ Confusingly, another actor called Brown – Faith Brown – is also famous for a Margaret Thatcher impression. You can't have too many, though. Impressions of Margaret Thatcher, I mean. But also actors called Brown.

I feel I must relay a story I heard about the shoot for *Wombling Free* – although being a mere background operative, I wasn't there, of course, and cannot vouch for its veracity. So perhaps take the following with a pinch of the usual.

Anyway the story goes that at one of the locations for the shoot, which, coincidentally, were in my current neck of the woods in Buckinghamshire, members of the crew one night held an outdoor party. And the following morning the ground was rather besmirched by spent beer cans and plastic cups and other detritus, as the ground often will be after gatherings of a convivial nature.

So the owner of the property, who was not best pleased, gathered all the rubbish in a sack and, by way of making his feelings clear, tipped the contents of the sack over the roof of Lionel Jeffries's car.

Which, of course, in the context of a movie about the litter-gathering Wombles, and their avowed mission to make good use of the things that they find, things that the everyday folk leave behind . . . well, that sackful over the car roof becomes an even more pointed response.

Truth or mischief? Reader, I'll let you be the judge. Good story, though.

As for my own part in the confection of this Wombling entertainment, alas I seem to recall nothing of any substance. Taking place, for the most part, in windowless studios around a bare microphone, those voice-over sessions do rather blend into one another at this distance – even if, as in this case, that windowless studio must have been within the hallowed portals of Pinewood Studios. I don't think we left any litter behind us, though.

And was there eventually a glamorous premiere for *Wombling Free* in the heart of London's West End at which, raffishly besuited, I sashayed with a modest smile along the red carpet, pausing only to acknowledge the screams of acclaim from the gathered fans?

Reader, if that were so, then time has pulled its weighty eiderdown entirely over memory's rumpled bedsheets in this matter, and I no longer recall a single thing about it. To be perfectly honest, I can't even remember how the movie ends, though I suspect it's happily and with lots of litter getting picked up. That's just a hunch, though.

But never mind the details. The point is, the history books will show that, at the peak of Womblemania, I was part of the Womble story – and nobody can take that away from me.

However . . . enough Wombling. Back to the diary.

Monday 5 March, Murder in a Bad Light, Brighton.

No, no, nothing untoward here. Just the opening night of a touring production of a comedy thriller by Dave Freeman, starring John Bird, Terry Scott and Dilys Lane, at Brighton's Theatre Royal. I must have dashed down to the south coast to support my fellow professionals, and perhaps to venture backstage afterwards and congratulate them on their work with that bomb-proof line for such occasions: 'Darling, you've done it again!'*

Incidentally, the diary entry for the following day states, baldly: *Ronnie Barker (Hodder), 47 Bedford Square*. I can only imagine, given the reference to a publisher, Hodder, and a posh address in Fitzrovia, that this was one of Ronnie's book launches, most likely for *Gentleman's Relish*, the follow-up to the bestselling *Sauce*, and another of Ronnie's collections of antique bawdiness, on which subject he was acknowledged to be a world-leading expert.

From opening night to book launch . . . why, my life was a dizzying whirl through society's upper echelons in those days, and no mistaking. Although, looking more closely, there don't seem to be any other first nights or book launches recorded in this diary, or much room for them. So clearly my life was a dizzying whirl through society's upper echelons, but solely between Monday 5 March and Tuesday 6 March.

That said, there is this entry, later in the year:
Tuesday 2 October, No Sex Please Party, Embassy Club.

Again, please form no untoward impressions here. This will merely have been a gathering with friends and former colleagues from the West End farce *No Sex Please – We're British*, in which, a few years earlier, I had the honour of

---

* Never fails to paper over an awkward moment, that line, although another strong contender for use at such times is 'Darling, so brave!'

succeeding Michael Crawford in the leading role – my first big West End appointment.

Incredible to reflect that, at this point in my diary, *No Sex Please* still had another eight years to run, on its way to a record-busting total of 6,761 performances. That show had legs, and I've always been very proud to say that my legs were among them.

Monday 21 May, The Impressionists: 2 progs, Paris, 4.45.

Now, this was nothing to do with paintings – and nor, sadly, does 'Paris' here connote a little business trip to the capital of romance, delightful as such a thing might have been.

On the contrary, it denotes a quick scuttle down to Lower Regent Street and the Paris Theatre, a former cinema reconstituted as a recording studio, and one of the homes of BBC comedy.

And *The Impressionists*? Well, that was a now largely forgotten radio panel show, onto which I would have been invited to supply some of my fine (and you might almost say uncanny) vocal imitations – almost certainly my Jim Callaghan, and most likely my Harold Wilson as well.

Incidentally, this was on a day when (so the diary entry tells me) I'd already spent the morning at 'De Lane Lea Studio One' in Greek Street, making an advertisement for Webster's beer.

Was that one of the Yorkshire ale ads with the talking dray horses? Possibly it was. Was I myself a talking dray horse? I may well have been. Did I even get to speak the, at the time, widely known tagline: 'It's right tasty, is Webster's'? Again, perfectly possible.

But anyway, from a dray horse in the morning to the recently deposed Labour prime minister in the afternoon; just another day's vocal work for the jobbing actor about town in 1979.

What strikes me now, though, looking back, is just how much radio work I was doing in this period. Barely a week went by without me pitching up somewhere to help out on some comedy for someone who needed it.

There was *Marks in his Diary* on Radio 2, with the wonderfully lugubrious Alfred Marks, of whom it was said that he could stand on a stage and do nothing and people would laugh. And that's among the rarest of all talents, though harder to pull off in a radio studio. But, of course, he found ways to be extremely funny there, too, and it was a privilege to be alongside him while he was doing so.

Then there was *The News Huddlines*, with Roy Hudd. Roy was an extraordinary person to be around – a powerful comic performer, of course, but also a historian of comedy whose specialist subject was the variety era. He could regale you for hours with tales of obscure entertainers such as Juna the Human Gasometer, who could apparently ingest butane and then light lamps with his breath. And the juggler who used, not balls, nor even flaming torches, but live geese.

I forget the name of that one. The Great Gander? But it's

certainly an act I was glad to hear about, and would love to have seen, and maybe sheltered from.

And *The News Huddlines* was a phenomenon. It ran for fifty-one series, stretching from 1975 to 2001. It took the news of the day and toyed with it, though Roy would always say gently to anyone who came on: 'Don't pull the wings off the butterfly.' The show had some bite but nobody was ever getting completely chewed up, and its general sense of amiability and broad goodwill is probably why it survived as long as it did.

So I loved being part of that. But best of all for me was without question the satirical show *Week Ending* – pretty much a fixture in the gardener's diary in this period. Every Friday morning, I would leave my flat, walk a few blocks round the corner to the BBC, and descend to a studio in the bowels of Broadcasting House, there to indulge the precious liberty that we enjoy in this country: the freedom to take the mickey out of the government and sundry other figures of authority without being arrested for it.

To ensure maximum topicality, *Week Ending* was put together on the day of broadcast. That was a buzz in itself – walking in at the beginning of the day to a blank slate and leaving at the end with a finished show in the can. I loved being around the writers who were smart enough to turn that tight shift around – people like Jeffrey Atkinson, Clive Davidson and David Renwick. I loved working with talented and astonishingly versatile cast members like Sheila Steafel and David Tate and Bill Wallis, whose Harold Wilson was, I will concede, superior to mine. And I loved working with the producer David Hatch, who went on to become a dear friend. At that time he quite often seemed to be getting summoned upstairs for a dressing-down from the BBC's honchos about overstepping the mark in some manner, but never seemed too perturbed about it.

It wasn't the most fashionable thing to be doing at that moment in history, by any stretch, and it certainly wasn't a gig which seemed likely to bring me fame and riches untold. Yet reporting for duty on that show was a thrill as far as I was concerned – a satisfaction of an altogether different order, if you don't mind me saying so, from reporting for duty on *Blankety Blank*, as superficially glitzy as that might have been.

And when I think about why doing radio comedy should have meant so much to me – should have felt like the heart of things in so many ways – the answer isn't hard to find. It's the connection it has with the past and my childhood. It routes me right back to where I came from – to the back room in the house that I grew up in.

Something the writer David Nobbs once said about the effect of listening to radio shows with his family as a child really rang true with me. He described his family as 'close-knit' and yet he admitted that they never really talked about love and affection with each other at all. But what they did do was sit together and listen to comedy on the radio. 'Our shared laughter round the snug coal fire spoke of those things for us,' David said.

Similarly, my parents were not especially demonstrative, physically or verbally. Certainly my father wasn't. There wasn't much hugging going on in our Lodge Lane house, the way we tend to be with each other now.

My parents weren't exceptional in that, though. It was just how people generally were at the time. And that didn't mean love and affection weren't present. You simply felt the presence of those things in other ways. And sitting in the back room in the evening, or at Sunday lunchtimes, with the radio on, and sharing comedy together was one of the biggest of those ways.

It was *Life with the Lyons* and *It's That Man Again* and Kenneth Horne with Kenneth Williams in *Beyond Our Ken* and anything with Peter Ustinov in it. It was all those golden products of the post-war radio comedy boom. And it was *The Goon Show* too, of course, although I'm not sure my father entirely shared my love for them. There was a lot of madness and anarchy in the Goons that possibly called most loudly to the younger ones among us. But I was just shy of my eleventh birthday when *The Goon Show* launched onto the airwaves, in May 1951, and I utterly adored them from the beginning.

'Me eyes ain't what they used to be. No, they used to be me ears.'

What did that even mean? I had no idea, really, and still don't. All I knew was that these lines zinging out of the radio in stupid voices had the power to cause absurd images to form in your head and make you laugh. The Goons gave us bizarre tales of 'The Phantom Head-Shaver' and 'The Dreaded Batter-Pudding Hurler' and I don't think I'd ever laughed so hard and so consistently at anything in my life.

It's not clear if the BBC quite understood what they had on their hands here. There was more than a little starchiness in the air in those days, and the Corporation weren't even sure they should be using the word 'Goons' in polite society.* There's a story that at one meeting about the show a senior BBC executive asked, 'What is this *Go On Show*?' Initially the bigwigs wanted to put it out under the winsome title *The Junior Crazy Gang*.

The Goons fought that and managed to win a compromise in which the show went out for its first series under the title *Crazy People, featuring Radio's Own Crazy Gang, the Goons*. Which, whatever else you want to say about it, didn't exactly trip off the tongue.

The fight continued, and for the second series, it became *The Goon Show, featuring Those Crazy People* – better, but still cumbersome. Only for series three was it allowed to stand proud as *The Goon Show*.

* And wait until you find out how the post-war BBC felt about the word 'drawers'. We'll be discussing their high-minded principles in this area in a later chapter.

This time, thirty-five years ago – half a lifetime. This photo from the
Only Fools and Horses 'The Jolly Boys' Outing' special really takes me
back. It was taken somewhere in Margate in the summer of 1989.
What a band of utterly loveable fools we were.

Credit: Trinity Mirror/Mirrorpix/Alamy Stock Photo

Eight years later … here I am at the National Television Awards in
1997 with Nick Lyndhurst and Buster Merryfield. I picked up an
award for 'Most Popular Comedy Performance' for *Only Fools and
Horses* and we also won 'Most Popular Comedy Series'. I was thrilled
to win 'Most Popular Actor' for *A Touch of Frost* too. I'm not sure
what the other award was for but it was such a special night.

This time, every year: the *Only Fools and Horses* conventions. I eagerly look forward to them now (having initially been reluctant). This brilliant crew and the chance to move among the show's remarkable and ever-loyal fans and hear their tales makes it all worthwhile. You can just about see me in the middle.

Before I was known for Derek Trotter, one of my 'big breaks' came in the 1967 children's comedy show *Do Not Adjust Your Set*, starring alongside Denise Coffey and members of the Monty Python team: Terry Jones, Eric Idle and Michael Palin. Whatever happened to them? It was produced by the wonderful Humphrey Barclay, a dear friend to this day.

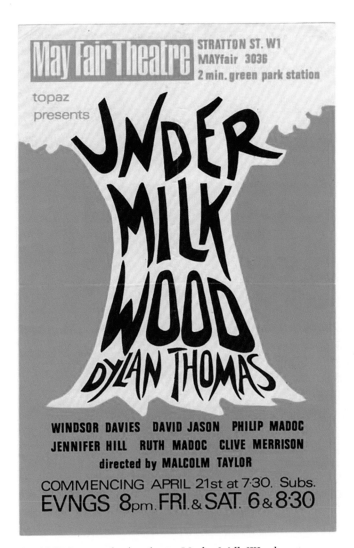

In 1967 I was asked to be in *Under Milk Wood*, written by Dylan Thomas. Over the next four years I would appear in a number of productions of the play. Dylan Thomas's wonderful Welsh phrasings have rung repeatedly and resonantly throughout my life.

It was once my great good fortune to secure the part of Skullion the head porter in Channel 4's 1987 adaptation of Tom Sharpe's novel *Porterhouse Blue*.

Me fooling around with the cast of *Under Milk Wood*.

This photo was taken during the 1960s when I was with the Manor Players amateur dramatics group.

Another photo from the Manor Players – this one from a production of *The Teahouse of the August Moon* by John Patrick, based on the 1951 novel by Vern Sneider. I was playing a range of parts at a young age, and the plays had excellent production values. It was a great way to build up my acting skills.

Ronnie Barker and me during *Open All Hours*. Ronnie Barker was different. He had an instinct for comedy, certainly, but he also had something which, in our business, is far rarer: an equal instinct for generosity. He really was a teacher. He could share what he knew, and he did so. And he could make space for the people around him to be funny, too.

With two of my heroes, Ronnie Barker and Richard Attenborough, receiving a BAFTA Fellowship in 2003. Life doesn't get much better for an actor.

Lesson there for all artists: stick to your guns and you may get your own way eventually.

So I instantly and lastingly loved *The Goons*, and marvelled at the magic that could bring this kind of pleasure into your home over the airwaves. But imagine the thrill when I discovered that this stuff was being created not all that far south of where we lived.

The Goons would also do a lot of their recording in the aforementioned Paris Theatre, but they also used the Camden Palace Theatre on Camden High Street. What's more, tickets to see them do their recordings cost *nothing*. Incredibly, you just had to write off to the BBC and ask for them.

So me and my mate Micky Weedon did just that. I don't think either of us thought we'd be successful: surely everyone in the world wanted to go and see *The Goon Show* being recorded. Yet a miracle occurred: back came our stamped addressed envelope with two tickets inside it.

And off we went, one Sunday night. The Camden Palace Theatre was an old music-hall venue which had been only minimally adjusted on its way to becoming a BBC recording facility. The seats had been stripped out of the stalls to make room for the orchestra which all BBC light-entertainment programmes required in those days. So we sat up in the circle, looking down on the musicians in the band and beyond them, in a haphazard tangle of wires and microphones, the stage area. And then quite late, at 9.15 p.m., the recording began.

Michael Bentine had left the show by then, taking with him the mad scientist character that he played, Captain Osric Pureheart, who had been one of my earliest favourites. So that was a little sad.

Incidentally, just like Ronnie Barker (who was another huge fan of *The Goons*, an influence and a passion we shared), Michael Bentine was a great frequenter of antique shops and junk stalls. His son, Richard, once recalled coming home and discovering, plonked in the middle of the sitting room, a brown leather saddle mounted on a big metal frame. And on top of that saddle was his father, watching a John Wayne movie on the television.

This was Bentine's latest junk-shop find – and very pleased with it he appeared to be, too. However, the saddle did not survive the arrival home of Bentine's wife. Despite his protests about how the saddle offered an extraordinarily comfortable seating position for television viewing – not to mention a highly appropriate one if a western happened to be on – out it went.

I raise all this merely to point out how comical eccentricity isn't always just something that people concoct for the cameras or the microphones. Sometimes it dwells in the bones.

But Bentine was gone – he'd ridden his saddle into the sunset, you could say – and I saw the Goons when they were a trio: Harry Secombe, Spike Milligan and Peter Sellers. Two things made a huge impression on me that night.

Firstly – and this was fantastically compelling to watch – the three of them were constantly suppressing their own laughter. They were having as good a time as the rest of us, and fooling around with each other (and with the audience) way beyond the boundaries of the script, in as much as the script had any boundaries.

Apparently, the constant challenge with *The Goons* when the programmes reached the editing stage was cutting out the laughter that had erupted from the audience at the sight of something one of the cast had randomly done – laughter which had nothing to do with anything going on in the script and which would make no sense to the listener hearing the show 'blind' at the point of broadcast. Having witnessed them in action, I can imagine how that editing job must have approached the complexity of Swiss watch-mending.

The second thing that stayed with me was the way Peter Sellers didn't just stand there at the microphone and read the script, which is what you might have casually imagined was happening during a radio recording. On the contrary, he seemed to be in constant motion.

Whether he was voicing the part of Hercules Grytpype-Thynne, or Major Bloodnok, or Bluebottle (the squeaky-voiced Boy Scout originally known as Ernie Splutmuscle), or Henry Crun, or whichever of the mad cast of characters it happened to be, Sellers's shoulders would be involved, his chest, his legs . . . He was right inside those characters.

It was a physical thing. Inhabiting those people changed

the shape, not just of his mouth and his face, but of his whole body. That was a real lesson to me about voice work and acting on the radio. It's easy to forget this, if you're not on a stage in front of people, or on camera, but a disembodied voice is no voice at all. Voices always come from *somewhere*.

I'm absolutely sure I had never set eyes on Sellers before that night. He was a radio star as far as I was concerned, and radio stars in those days were simply invisible. But having set eyes on him I was a fan for good. I bought the album he later released, *Songs for Swingin' Sellers*, and played it until I practically wore the grooves off it. It was produced by George Martin, who would go on to know far broader fame for other things. But that Sellers record came into my life at Christmas 1959, when I was nineteen, and meant more to me than any subsequent record by the Beatles – for its musical spoofs and sketches, of course, but even its sleeve notes – 'only use needles of Burmese plywood' – were irresistibly funny to me. Like everything Sellers touched, it seemed.

As I sat in that seat in the circle, drinking it all in, the idea that at any point in the future there would be a thread connecting me to any of the stars on that stage would have seemed as surreal as any of the bits of madness they were coming out with – an entirely preposterous concept.

And yet that thread exists. OK, it's not the strongest thread you've ever come across and you probably wouldn't want to sew a split in your trousers with it . . . but I'm still fiercely proud of it.

Because years later, Ronnie B collaborated with Spike Milligan to produce 'The Phantom Raspberry Blower of London Town', a spoof Gothic tale whose roots in the work of the Goons could be detected in its title, and which at one point ran as a weekly series of short episodes inserted into *The Two Ronnies*.

And the supplier of the loud raspberries blown to terrorise the populace by that menace of the streets?

Well, in fact there were two. Spike himself did some of them. But the other blower was me, a duty entrusted to me by Ronnie B, a long-time admirer, I have to tell you, of my work in the raspberry-blowing arena.

You take your praise where you find it. The point is, yes, Branagh has his Hamlet and McKellen has his Lear. But without wishing to blow my own trumpet here, or even to blow my own raspberry, I will forever more have the satisfaction of knowing that my raspberries were once deemed fit to flutter in the breeze alongside Spike Milligan's. That's a mighty accolade for me, it really is.

Anyway, all this is by way of saying that it was around the radio that I first understood just how binding comedy could be, how it could play a part in family life, how it could bring people together and make them feel close to one another. And I can see how that's true, in a different era and in a different medium, for *Only Fools and Horses*, too.

Because, yes, it was just a comedy show in which people dressed up and stomped around the place saying and doing daft things. But at the same time it arrived in people's homes and it became this thing around which people gathered. It got knitted into the fabric of people's lives for a while, and from what I can tell, in many, many cases it remains there. And if you ever get to help put a show like that together you can consider yourself a very lucky person.

But all that was off in the distance for me in 1979. And I sometimes think, if things had worked out differently, if television had never taken off for me and I had only had radio, I could have been content with that.

However, on the subject of television . . . well, clearly, amid all the radio shows and the voice-over work and the constant buzzing of my pager that were filling 1979, that struggle for lift-off in my TV career continued. In fact, I seemed to be making some rather exciting headway in that department. At any rate, my trusty gardener's diary also records the setting aside of a block of time in the early summer for shooting series three of *A Sharp Intake of Breath*.

Yes, miracle of miracles, after all the various travails recorded in the previous chapter, I had finally found myself starring in a sitcom which had lasted beyond its first series. Was this, then, going to be the big one – the show that transformed my professional fortunes once and for all? Or was fate going to perform its usual dampening of the crisps and leave me thwarted again?

Reader, can you guess?

A Sharp Intake of Breath started life as a one-off piece in a series called *The Sound of Laughter*, a compendium of half-hour comedies put together in 1977 and broadcast one per week, which was a popular way of testing ideas back then. This was how *Porridge* and *Open All Hours* got going, too. Essentially you had half an hour to run your comedy idea up a nationally visible flagpole and find out if anybody wanted to salute it.

These inter-pilot contests were obviously a bit of a lottery. They certainly weren't a watertight way to test sitcoms for durability because . . . well, you only got half an hour. But also, inevitably there was a bit of judging the shows in relation to each other rather than on their own merits. If your show happened to go out the week after a real peach which had got people talking, you were probably in trouble.

Nevertheless, I rather enjoyed the arrangement. In a way, it sent me all the way back to the point at which I came in – victory in the 1954 East Finchley Drama Festival for Northside Secondary Modern School and their production of the Civil War play *Wayside War*, featuring me in a large floppy hat and brandishing a sword.

No harm in a bit of competition, clearly.

That was the point I realised that acting could bring a person not just the acclaim of his peers and their parents, but also, on top of that, a little silver medal, nailed to a block of wood. Obviously not real silver but an award nevertheless. It was for best supporting player and I still have it.

Such treasure! For my fourteen-year-old mind, I think

that rather swung it, acting-wise. Before this breakthrough, I hadn't been sure that larking about onstage in costume was the kind of thing a wannabe Jack the Lad such as myself should be getting involved in – or certainly not if he wanted to maintain his standing among his genuine Jack the Lad peers.

But after that, you could never keep me away from the dressing-up box and the make-up table, so totally and help-lessly entranced was I by the sheer captivating magic of the dramatic arts.

Or maybe not. It seems I still wasn't *entirely* persuaded of the virtues of a thespian path, even by the glitter of a medal at fourteen. At any rate, soon after that legendary triumph in East Finchley, a man called Doug Weatherhead, who ran the Incognito Theatre Group in Friern Barnet, cornered me and my aforementioned *Goon*-loving friend Micky Weedon, who had shared the stage with me in that award-winning production, and asked us if we'd ever con-sidered giving any of our spare evenings to the am-dram cause.

And, even as veterans of that famous East Finchley vic-tory, the instinctive reaction of Micky and me alike was to make clear to this Mr Weatherhead that no, we hadn't con-sidered it, and that no, we wouldn't consider it – perhaps even at the same time adding a slightly leering expression to our faces as if to say, 'Are you kidding?'

Then Doug mentioned in passing the fact that the group

was almost entirely made up of girls. About twenty of them, in fact.

Cut to the following Monday evening. And who are these two young figures that we now see cycling as fast up Torrington Park in the direction of the Incogs' base in Holly Park Road as they had ever cycled anywhere?

That'll be me and Micky Weedon, of course. Because where else were we going to find ourselves in a room containing twenty girls and no other male rivals for their attention, apart from in our wildest dreams?

Look, what can I say? We were teenagers – even though teenagers were still a couple of years from being invented at that point. But thus does nature take its course, and such are the bare animal motives which in no small way shape our destinies and the journeys of our lives. And thanks in some measure to that unsubtle impulse, acted upon in the hot folly of youth, I became an actor.

So, anyway, now here I was, a couple of decades later, seeing if I could finally get a sitcom away, after several years of failing to do so, and rather relishing the competitive challenge. Looking down the list of the other runners and riders in *The Sound of Laughter* steeplechase, I didn't know what to think about our chances really. We were going to be first out of the traps, the first show on air, which might help the cause.

But we were also going up against an item called *Young at Heart* which was going to feature the legendary British actor John Mills in his first sitcom role. Hard not to think that would be a contender when the medals – or rather the commissions – were being handed out.*

As for *After the Boom was Over* (Jonathan Pryce and Gabrielle Lloyd in a piece about a young couple trying to buy a house) or *What a Performance* with Robin Bailey, Noel Davis and Rosemary Martin, or something called *Bricks Without Straw* with Michael Elphick . . . well, it was just impossible to know, really.†

A Sharp Intake of Breath was written by a lovely guy called Ronnie Taylor, who had a very colourful CV: a sitcom for Leslie Crowther and Sylvia Syms, a lot of writing for the comedian Harry Worth, and a directing job on the first ever British series of *Candid Camera*.

Ronnie's pilot episode was about a man trying to get a porch built over his back door and having run-ins with the builder. Typical sitcom material, you could say, but there was a nice little twist. My character, Peter, broke the fourth wall, as we say – meaning he would occasionally break off from engaging with the other characters in the scene, look into the camera and talk to the viewer directly.

It was a way for the character to take the audience into his

---

* *Young at Heart* with John Mills and Megs Jenkins would indeed be commissioned for three series between 1980 and 1982 by ATV on the strength of this showing.
† To the very best of my knowledge, none of these shows travelled beyond the thirty-minute pilot stage of the journey.

confidence and, for a comedy designed to hit prime time on ITV in 1977, it felt like a pretty radical move. Oh yes – I was ahead of Phoebe Waller-Bridge in *Fleabag* by several decades there, with my fourth-wall-breaking.

And as for the very recent claim of the BBC's head of comedy, no less – made in an interview in June 2024 – that the fourth-wall-breaking in *Mrs Brown's Boys* was, when it came along in 2011, 'something a bit different with the form' . . . well, I'm sure what he meant to say was that it was something a bit different from the different thing that we did with it more than thirty years before that in *A Sharp Intake*.

Slip of the tongue, there, I don't doubt, on the part of the head of comedy.

Anyhow, in the role of Peter's wife, Sheila, was the excellent Patricia Brake – not the first time we'd worked on a show together. Patricia had played Ingrid, Norman Stanley Fletcher's daughter in *Porridge*, a part which naturally got bigger in the spin-off series *Going Straight*, which showed Ronnie's Fletch trying to adapt to life outside prison.

And, incidentally, while I'm mentioning it, in the role of Raymond, Ingrid's brother in *Going Straight*, was a seventeen-year-old actor widely held to be showing great promise, called Nicholas Lyndhurst.

Now, I wonder what became of *him*.

Also on board for *A Sharp Intake*, as Peter's father-in-law, and artificially greyed-up for the role, was Richard Wilson, who was still a number of years away from occupying the role of Victor Meldrew in *One Foot in the Grave*.

Equally, then, Richard was still some years from the mixed blessing, known intimately to those of us who find ourselves associated with popular sitcoms, of being followed round the country by a catchphrase, and of hearing that catchphrase called out across streets, shops, car parks, restaurants etc.

A cheerful forbearance is strongly recommended in this situation, I believe, and the sitcom actor who finds himself or herself a magnet for this kind of action does well to remember that there are almost certainly far worse things to have shouted at you in the street than a line from a show you have been in.

However, in Richard's case the problem must have been especially acute because the phrase most strongly associated with him loaned itself so perfectly to a stranger's greeting: 'I don't believe it!' So, in fairness, who could resist?

Richard's traditional reply, though, was a good one: 'You'd better.'

Incidentally, here's another example of casting's fickleness: it seems that Richard was not straightforwardly the first choice for that eventually legendary part. Apparently the producers had Les Dawson in the mix at one stage, but Les was hesitant about it for some reason.

From this point in history, of course, you can't think of the decision going any other way, so completely did Richard come to embody the character. But as I say, such is the brittle nature of casting. On another day, with another kind of wind blowing, and with someone in the office in another mood . . . well, the whole story of comedy gets rewritten, and people end up shouting 'I don't believe it!' at Les Dawson rather than Richard Wilson.

And I speak, of course, as someone who was, as I understand it, at least fourth, and possibly even fifth, choice to play Derek Trotter. Now (and I'm sure Richard would agree with me here), you can choose to dwell on such things and feel hurt and affronted and generally get the hump about the world's failure to recognise your talents *instantly*, over and above the claims of all others, and beat a path directly to your door.

But hard-won wisdom suggest that it's much better, surely, to save yourself the grief by letting it all wash through, on the grounds that there are all sorts of random forces at work at these casting moments over which you can exercise no control.

The truth is, it doesn't matter where you are in the queue, because you can't do much about that. It only matters what you do when you get to the front. Because that bit *is* in your power.

Anyway, it all came together on the night for our pilot, and A *Sharp Intake* was duly commissioned. Patricia wasn't available to do the series, sadly, but in came Jacqueline Clarke, who proved to be a perfect replacement and the show quite quickly started to shape up.

Ronnie Taylor had a real gift for spinning comedy gold from mundanity – the tiny irritations and the little tribulations of daily life that people would instantly recognise and relate to. Things like waiting in for the gas man; trying to book a summer holiday; finding your car won't start.* Over the next couple of years, we made two six-episode series which went over pretty well.

And because the show had time to unfold, a chemistry evolved. Ronnie began to write with me in mind, and to create situations in which he knew I could be funny. This was the first time I'd had that relationship on a show I was starring in – the first time I'd been playing in something where the writing and the acting were coming together in unison. It was like a light going on: 'So *this* is how it works.' I could see the show lasting a long time and maybe building a real momentum.

But then disaster, right out of the blue. One minute I was hearing that Ronnie had been taken suddenly ill. And I wasn't thinking too much of it, because he was only

---

* The scenario in which you find your car won't start is the only example here that perhaps dates the show a touch. These days cars tend to start when you ask them to. It's one of the ways in which we can indisputably claim that life has got better in the last fifty years. Accordingly it's easy to forget that, back then, the possibility that your car would let you down – mostly on account of being 'cold' – was necessarily in your mind almost every time you went out to it in the morning. And don't get me started on the 'choke'. Nobody misses the 'choke'.

fifty-eight, so surely he was going to be OK. And the next minute I was hearing that he had died.

It was just so shocking. Fifty-eight: no age at all. That was the first time I'd had that experience on a show – of reality crashing in and bursting the little light-entertainment bubble that we were all cheerfully going around in. Sadly it would not be the last time.

At that point, Ronnie had written three of the proposed six episodes for series three of *A Sharp Intake*, so we made those in 1979, as my diary records, and they went out as a shortened series at the start of 1980. They were, in my opinion, the strongest and funniest of all the episodes, because that was the direction the series was heading in.

The very last of them was an episode with the lovely title 'Look Who's Coming For Ever', in which, in an attempt to bond with his father-in-law, Peter heads out onto the golf course with him. This episode therefore records a very rare encounter between me and a bag of golf clubs.

Peter is a golfing novice who is trying to pretend that he isn't, a role which didn't require much acting on my part. At one point I find myself getting practically throttled by Richard Wilson, who is trying to sort out my posture over the ball, grabbing hold of me and twisting my head into place.

I'm not sure Richard knew one end of a golf club from the other any more than I did. That said, he is Scottish and putters tend to be issued at birth up there, so I may be doing him a huge disservice here. But he certainly did a good *impression* of someone who knew a five iron from a sand wedge. For me, then as now, a sand wedge was only ever going to be lunch.

However, please note: I do eventually get the ball away in that scene. In fact, I swing through quite nicely and give it a right old clout, connecting very sweetly if I may say so, and indicating an instinctive feel for the game that might have yielded sizeable rewards had I ever chosen to develop my interest in the sport in the longer term.

I won't tell you how many takes were involved, though.

Or where the ball eventually flew to. I don't think it was ever found.

Later in that segment, in a scene somewhat redolent of a famous advertisement for Hamlet cigars, I am shown in a self-created shower of sand, drastically failing to get my ball out of a bunker – and then drastically failing to get myself out of the bunker, too. I'm left sliding up and down the bunker's steep banks while the game moves on. It was a funny episode and a nice one to remember Ronnie Taylor by.

But, oh, the frustration – the sense of loss and the sense of incompletion.

I assumed the show wouldn't continue without Ronnie. But a little while passed and the following year a decision was taken at ITV to rekindle the series for a fourth run. The writing was taken over by Vince Powell, who had a whole string of seventies sitcom successes behind him, many created in partnership with Harry Driver, including *Bless*

This House. Powell wrote six new episodes of *A Sharp Intake* which were eventually broadcast in 1981.

At the same time, shaking things up still further, Les Chatfield left as director and Stuart Allen came in. New writer, new director . . . I guess you could say there was a touch of Trigger's Broom about this project. If you changed all those bits, was it even the same show?

Now, I guess Trig would have said it was, but then I'm not sure he's the first person you'd want on your side during an argument of an abstract philosophical nature. Certainly I felt the show's set-up now had a wholly different energy, and it made me a little uneasy from the off.

The first of those new episodes had Peter, my character, acquiring a flashy Mercedes, taking it for a drive and getting into an argument with a group of anti-pollution protesters who were blocking the road. This was filmed in 1980, remember, but it would seem highly topical now, of course.

Anyway, if I remember rightly, the story ended with absolutely everybody getting arrested. Which was quite funny, maybe. But it was funny in a different way from the way in which the show had been funny before. It seemed bigger, louder. Ronnie's quieter touch was gone.

By the end of the series, we had veered into the realms of the Alfred Hitchcock spoof with an episode titled 'Rear Window', which found Peter laid up in bed with a sprained ankle and wondering, as he stares idly out of the window, whether his neighbour is a murderer. It was very tidily written, and there were laughs to be had. But again there was this larger scale to everything, somehow. By then my faith in the show had quietly evaporated. It was a different kind of comedy and I felt that we had moved away from the interest in tiny things that originally made it special.

ITV may have thought so too. *A Sharp Intake of Breath* never returned.

Remember that list of false dawns in the previous chapter? Chalk this one up as another.

So that, more or less, was me in 1979 – a man with a dream that seemed to be trembling like a candle in a force 10 gale, a copy of the *Sunday Telegraph* Gardener's Diary in his jacket pocket, and a slightly worried expression on his face. The age of forty was no longer a rumour, it was fast approaching – and I still had no idea if the big break was ever going to come my way.

But I did know that I was busy. The slimline diary told me that much. And maybe if I could just stay busy, and keep myself in the game, something big would eventually come along.

CHAPTER THREE

*Of plonkers, bust-ups, and the slings and
arrows of outrageous news reporting*

Here's a worrying thought I've been forced to confront
this very morning over breakfast: are we about to run
out of plonkers?

I know – it's a hard idea to get your head around. Only
yesterday you would have said plonkers were in plentiful
supply. The world seemed plonker-rich. More plonkers than
you could shake a stick at, you might even have felt. It was
certainly hard to imagine a time would ever come when
there might not be any plonkers at all.

But the news is all over the morning papers, which Strobes,
my wrinkled retainer, has, as usual, brought up from the gate-
house and carefully ironed in the laundry, before depositing
them in a precise fan-shape here in the breakfast room, on
the tablecloth beside the toast rack.

According to language experts – people with their ears
to the ground, and maybe with their ears to the walls, as

well – the word 'plonker' is on the wane. Apparently there has been a distinct falling-off in the use of the term. The nation's young just aren't reaching for it as their insult of choice in the way people once did. These days plonkers are more likely to find themselves being called something a bit more modern, such as 'basic', or 'lame'.

'Have you seen this, Strobes?' I say, brandishing a knife loaded with marmalade. 'We're running out of plonkers.'

Strobes is over at the sideboard, placing the silver tureen of kedgeree on the hotplate.

'It does indeed seem hard to imagine, sir,' he quietly replies without looking up.

He can be very dry sometimes, Strobes. I must have a word with him about that.

Anyway, the story really is everywhere, from *The Times* ('Basic reason Gen Z won't be calling you a plonker') to the *Daily Star*, which goes with the towering front-page headline 'THE END OF THE PLONKERS'.

'Younger generation turn nose up at our put-downs,' says the *Star*'s sub-heading. It goes on to say: 'Some of the best words in the English language like "plonker" and "git" are dying out because plonkers and gits don't know what they mean.'

Succinctly phrased, that – as you'd expect from an organ of record such as the *Star*.

And whose faces have been used to illustrate this urgent news item?

I suspect you can guess.

Staring out from the front page are Derek and Rodney Trotter, looking worried outside a phone box.

Oh, how proud my dear departed mother would have been. 'I'm in the paper, Mum.'

'Oh, that's nice, son. What does it say?'

'That it's the end of the plonker.'

But never mind that – this is troubling news, if true. And also under threat, it seems: the terms 'nitwit', 'numpty' and 'berk'. And as for 'nerk', 'dingbat' and 'wally-brain' . . . well, the stories don't actually mention those ones, but it can't be good news, can it? I mean, if the scrapheap beckons for 'plonker', the future can hardly be looking bright for 'dingbat', surely.

And whither 'twonk'?

Anyhow, it's 'plonker' everybody seems most concerned about. The implication is that the time may not be far ahead when you call someone a plonker and get nothing for your trouble except a blank look.

Which, of course, you might have been expecting and might have been part of the reason you called them a plonker in the first place . . .

Still, point taken. According to the research, one in four young people in 2024 had never heard the term 'plonker' and only one in five said they would feel offended if you came right out with it and called them one to their face. As far as the rest were concerned, you might as well be speaking French.

Which Derek Trotter also did, of course, and sometimes when he was trying to be insulting. But that's another matter, which we'll come on to later.

Now, as someone whose allotted time on this earth has been (through no prior planning of my own, I should say) intimately bound up with the word 'plonker' and its usage, you would perhaps expect me to have a view here. And, yes, I suppose I do – although I find it calming, on this as on so many matters, to seek the broader perspective.

As the popularity of a dearly loved insult allegedly diminishes before our sorrowful eyes, let us remember that this is the kind of thing that has been happening to insults for as long as insults have existed. Language is continually evolving and, as history is forever reminding us, it is not just the people of Margate who are cast upon time's ever-shifting sands.

Permit me to demonstrate. Just as soon as breakfast was cleared away, I instructed Strobes to fetch the library steps and take down from one of the higher shelves my well-thumbed copy of Francis Grose's great work from 1785, *A Classical Dictionary of the Vulgar Tongue*. And from this volume, I now pluck at random the following great eighteenth-century insults which are no longer really with us, here in 2024, and certainly seldom heard in the streets, pubs or workplaces of our wonderful homeland:

'addle-pate' (a muddle-headed or inconsiderate person)
'bull calf' (a person of great clumsiness)

'blunderbuss' (a person who is possibly even more clumsy than a bull calf, if you can imagine such a thing)

'duke-of-limbs' (a gangly individual – would possibly have suited an eighteenth-century Rodney, come to think of it)

and, my absolute favourite:

'death's head upon a mop stick' (pretty self-explanatory, and also quite good for Rodney).

All of those would, I don't doubt, have been highly satisfying words to sling in a deserving person's direction in their time. And all are no longer available to be slung, apart from in historical dramas, e.g. *Bridgerton* (maybe).

Such is the way of things, though. Why, I'm very sure Shakespeare himself never imagined the day would come when you could call someone an 'elf-skin' and not have them know exactly how you felt about them. Yet it's a long time since I've heard that one thrown between feuding motorists.

Nor any of these beauties, for that matter, famously aimed in a bunch at the character of Falstaff in Shakespeare's *Henry IV, Part 2*:

'That trunk of humours, that bolting-hutch of beastliness, that swollen parcel of dropsies, that huge bombard of sack, that stuffed cloak-bag of guts, that roasted Manningtree ox with pudding in his belly . . .'

On the subject of Shakespearean insults, it was once my

great good fortune to secure the part of Skullion the head porter in the Channel 4 adaptation of Tom Sharpe's novel *Porterhouse Blue*.

'Was that the role for which you received a Best Actor BAFTA in 1988?' I hear you softly interrupt to ask. 'And would that possibly be the BAFTA to which Daphne, the Jason Towers under-housemaid, is even now applying the Mr Sheen and a soft cloth?'

And, well, yes, now that you mention it, I did indeed end up thus gloriously decorated for my performance in that production, and thank you for remembering – although, naturally, modesty forbids that I dwell on it here or even so much as mention it. So let's quietly set that little detail aside and get back to the book.

And let's also leave Daphne to her labours, or she'll never be done in time to re-tile the stable block.

But my point is, the name 'Skullion' was derived from a defunct insult. I looked all this up. It's from a fifteenth-century French word – '*escuillon*', meaning 'cleaning cloth', which became 'scullion' and then got flung (along with the cleaning cloth itself, most likely) in a demeaning manner at the poor old lowly servant with the ropiest jobs in the kitchen, and thereafter at anyone else who was deemed not to merit the greatest of respect.

Hundreds of years later, though, with the term fallen out of use, Tom Sharpe could cleverly pick it up, switch the 'c' for a 'k' and arrive at a perfect surname for the character he had created – who was, you might recall, a scheming, underhand operator, the humble servant of a Cambridge college, yet darkly but deftly wheedling his way upwards. (It was a lot of fun portraying all of that, needless to say.)

So, yes, language alters, words lose and gain meanings, and eternal life is guaranteed to no insult, even the very best of them. Refer to someone these days as a 'snollygoster' and people will . . . well, people will probably think you're a bit of a plonker, in fact. But in nineteenth-century America everyone would have simply nodded knowingly and carried on with what they were doing. (A 'snollygoster' is a politician of no fixed principles – or, I guess you could more simply say, a politician.)

Why, no doubt the ancient Romans would have been sad to see the demise of the freedom they enjoyed to call someone a 'sterculinum publicum' – literally, a public pile of poo in Latin. Yet that was another belter which duly ended up on language's dunghill somewhere along the way – where, perhaps, it always belonged.

I can't deny, though, that I would be a little sad to see plonker go. We go back, me and plonker. And plonker, too, goes back. Views on the term's origin differ a little. Some think it refers to a person who says or does daffy things because they are drunk on cheap wine, or 'plonk'. Others suggest (and this I can well believe, given the general drift of British humour) that it's a reference to the male member – as, indeed, while we're on the subject, is 'pillock'.

113

But the valuable thing about plonker is that, yes, it's defin-itely an insult – but it's also a term of endearment. It depends how you say it, of course, but most of the time it lands fondly. And for that reason alone, I think it's worth preserving.

Should we be taking action, then? Getting together with like-minded types and forming 'Save the Plonker' groups? Taking out ads on public transport: 'Do your bit for plonker conservation: call someone a plonker today'?

Well, if you don't mind I'll leave that to others for now. I feel I've more than played my part in this struggle, with all those episodes of *Only Fools*. I've already given. Frankly, if we're talking about services to plonkerdom, I don't think I could ever reasonably be accused of having underdone it. In a roundabout kind of way, I was knighted for it, don't you know.

Also, between you and me, I wonder whether this news of plonker's demise is a touch exaggerated. I'm no expert, of course, and my ears are neither to the ground nor the walls, but I've got a hunch that the word 'plonker' has got a few more years in it yet. After all, for as long as there are plonkers . . .

* * *

It's not just when language is at stake that *Only Fools* finds itself thrust onto the current affairs agenda. Indeed, it never ceases to amaze me how frequently I can open a paper and find Derek Trotter staring out at me, in the headlines again on account of the fact that . . . well, you name it: that the word 'plonker' is in the news, or that dodgy deals are in the news (and let's face it, dodgy deals are rarely *out* of the news), or that people dressed in superhero costumes are in the news, or even that chandeliers are in the news. All these years after the programme ended, there still seems to be a whole cluster of topics for which the media's first point of reference is *Only Fools*.

And let's not even bother to mention bar flaps in this context.

Sometimes people will attach a still or a clip from the show in response to a news story in order to send the story up, or make some kind of ribald comment on it, and they'll post it on Faceplant or Tuk-Shop or Twotter or some such.* Friends send these on to me and most often I'll have a smile at them and feel glad and proud that the old show is still so much in people's minds.

Just occasionally, though, I might think, 'Oooh . . . are you sure?'

I had one of those recently. In March 2024, a huge container ship struck one of the pillars of the bridge outside

---

* Are these the right words? I will concede that I'm not yet a great frequenter of the social media platforms. But it's never too late, and maybe one day soon you'll be seeing me on Instagroan, or whatever it's called. First of all, though, I need to finish learning how to operate the remote for the television. Once I've mastered that . . .

Baltimore harbour in the USA. The ship had lost power, it seems, and couldn't be steered. There's a good chance you saw what happened next because the images made news all around the world. Shaken by the impact, the bridge – all 366 metres of it – collapsed into the water.

Very soon after this happened, a friend sent over a little skit someone had put together in which the footage of that poor container ship coming to grief had been cut around a scene from the *Only Fools* Christmas special 'To Hull and Back'.

It was the scene, you might recall, where our intrepid adventurers are setting off for Holland in their borrowed tub, relying on Albert's slightly overestimated piloting skills, with Del urging Albert ('England's greatest little sailor since Nelson lost the Armada', let's not forget) to go right and Albert insisting the correct term is 'starboard' and Del saying 'Don't start all that Captain Birds Eye bloody cobblers', and so on and so forth. Meanwhile the boat cuts a zigzag path out of the worryingly busy harbour, striking at least one other vessel on the way through.

Incidentally, if we're talking about Del's unquenchable optimism and what we can take from it as we go about our humble lives, there's a wonderful instance of it in that episode – at the train station, before the boat sets sail, when Rodney arrives from London and discovers exactly who Del has appointed to be the ship's captain for this dodgy voyage.

'Albert?' says Rodney. 'Every boat he's ever set foot on has sunk.'

'Yeah,' replies Del. 'But his luck has got to change at some point, hasn't it?'

Which is Del's mindset in a nutshell. The odds might be entirely stacked against you – the whole of *history*, in fact, might be stacked against you. But at some point fate must surely smile.

Still, here were these scenes from 'To Hull and Back' intercut with images of that real-life disaster, and I have to say, I felt uneasy about it. What was in my mind was that six people, part of a maintenance crew who were working on the bridge at the time, lost their lives as a consequence of that collision. So maybe this wasn't quite in the best possible taste.

Was I overreacting? I mean, I'm certainly not suggesting that events in which people have met their end are forever removed from the realm of humour, because, well, for one thing that would be jokes about the *Titanic* well and truly sunk – including, I guess, the one I just inadvertently made in that very sentence.

I don't know. I still haven't worked out why I felt so uncertain about it. Maybe it was just seeing my own face involved. But I just felt, in that case, very sensitive.

It's a complicated matter, though, isn't it? What's acceptable to laugh at and when? Where are the limits? We seem to be especially bothered by this at the moment, with squabbles breaking out all over the place about what we should or shouldn't find funny.

But of course, this isn't a new battle for comedy, by any stretch. On the contrary, it's a battle that people trying to be funny have been having since the dawn of time – right since, probably, the first cave painter drew a cartoon of a deer being hunted with a spear and someone looked at it and said, 'Well, that's all very amusing for you, I'm sure, but it's not very funny for the deer.'

For some perspective on this matter, I own a glorious historical artefact that was gifted to me a little while ago by a producer I worked with. It's a small, slim hardback book, just a handful of pages long, but properly bound with a green cloth cover and franked across the top with the words 'PRIVATE AND CONFIDENTIAL'.

I would contend that there are few words in the English language more thrilling than those to find on the front of a document – and no words more likely to have you scurrying to open it immediately.

And one's prying eyes are well rewarded. For here is the 'BBC Variety Programmes Policy Guide for Writers & Producers, 1948'.

No, wait – I know it doesn't *sound* like the most exciting book in the world. But trust me, this is gold dust. This booklet contains the guidelines laid down just after the war by the BBC for the creators of comedy and light-entertainment shows, in accordance with the national broadcaster's standards at that moment.

And here, along with some guidance regarding the

potential 'traps for the unwary or inexperienced', and a stern reminder of the need for 'continued vigilance in matters of taste', are listed the 'principal taboos' as the BBC perceived them in 1948.

Let me at this point simply quote the book. Steel yourself, dear reader.

In a section strongly recommending the general avoidance of 'crudities, coarseness and innuendo', the BBC regulators declare an 'absolute ban' upon 'suggestive references' to any of the following:

Honeymoon couples
Chambermaids
Fig leaves
Prostitution
Ladies' underwear – e.g. winter draws on
Animal habits, e.g. rabbits
Lodgers
Commercial travellers.

Got all that? I'm not making any of this up, by the way. That list is exactly as the book supplies it, complete with the provision of those wonderfully po-faced examples: 'Ladies' underwear – e.g. winter draws on.'

No punning references, if you please, to the seasonal undergarments of the female sex. BBC standards will not permit it.

And no talking about what rabbits get up to, either. You couldn't be at it like rabbits on the BBC in 1948. Unless, I suppose, you were an actual rabbit, in which case presumably allowances would have been made.

Or maybe not, given the temper of the times.

Oh, and no jokes about lavatories. Which strikes me as an ambitious stipulation, given the British love for humour of a lavatorial nature, a love which extends back at least as far as Chaucer and no doubt further.

No khazi gags? Big hill for the BBC to climb there, I would gently propose. Indeed, a doomed enterprise, surely. My contention would be: you can possibly take the lavatory out of the British comedian's material, but you can never take the British comedian out of the lavatory. Still, the BBC in 1948 seemed determined to have a go.

Obviously, given that this is a publicly funded broadcasting operation, the guidelines are very tight on advertising – and, indeed, they remain so today. Fair enough. However, the booklet provides a handy list of trade names that have sunk so far into the language by 1948 that they can be regarded as generic terms and therefore be sprinkled with impunity through one's scripts, if one so wishes.

Such terms include:

Aspirin
Bakelite
Cellophane

Gramophone
Nylon
Vaseline

It strikes me, looking at that list, that you could use two or three of those to forge a pretty filthy joke if you were of a mind to, but the BBC in 1948 would definitely rather that you didn't.

I'm surprised not to find Hoover on that trade-name list: clearly a Hoover was not yet an entirely interchangeable term for a vacuum cleaner.*

But Spam is listed which means it's fine, in this brave new dawn for the post-war world, to call Spam Spam. It would be another twenty-two years before the famous *Monty Python* 'Spam' sketch was broadcast across the BBC's airwaves, but it's good to know that it would have passed muster in 1948, too.†

Naturally this document has some strong words to say about expletives – if that's not a contradiction. 'Generally speaking,' the book lectures us, 'the use of expletives and

---

* In fact, Vaseline and Hoover are both still registered trademarks, even though Hoover patented its first vacuum cleaner in 1908. There's been a lot of dust under the carpet since then, and no mistaking.

† This may be an over-abundance of caution on my part, but I feel I should clarify that 'Spam' here refers to compressed meat, of a kind generally found in tins, and not to unsolicited emails, which might be people's immediate inference nowadays. That's language playing its tricks again.

forceful language on the air can only be justified in a serious dramatic setting where the action of the play demands them.'

So, when it comes to swearing, it looks like drama gets a bit of a free pass, but comedy does not. Typical! Those of us who found ourselves on the comedy side of the BBC's entertainment divide would often be sucking our teeth about what drama was allowed to get away with that comedy wasn't.

And in a similar vein we would have a little moan every now and again about the size of the budgets that were given to 'serious' drama by comparison with the budgets set aside for the work of we humble comics. Not only were they allowed to swear, they were given more money to swear with! But don't get me started on that . . .

Instead, let us run a wary eye over the list of proscribed terms for the prospective light entertainer on a national platform in 1948 – those words that must be avoided at all cost for fear of frightening those of a sensitive nature, not to mention their horses.

And, friendly reader, at this point I must urge you to put your hands over your ears, and over your eyes as well if you can manage it, because things are about to get spicy.

Indeed, consider the above paragraph a trigger warning.*

Here's the book again:

* Note that a trigger warning is a very different thing from a Trigger warning. A Trigger warning could almost certainly be safely ignored.

All such words as God, Good God, My God, Blast, Hell, Damn, Bloody, Gorblimey, Ruddy, etc. etc., should be deleted from scripts and innocuous expressions substituted.

Still with me? Or have you dropped this book into your lap in shock and taken to fanning your heated face with a perfumed hanky?

Things certainly change, don't they? It's true that there are still people these days who prefer not to hear the Lord's name taken in vain, and all respect to them. But the idea nowadays of substituting 'innocuous expressions' for the other items on that list . . . well, it would be a bit tricky, wouldn't it, because these days 'blast', 'hell' and 'damn' ARE the innocuous substitutions.

Much as a gently punning reference to 'winter draws on' seems like a harmlessly gentle joke to our modern ears, so it's difficult to imagine anybody getting upset in 2024 by the use of the expletive 'ruddy'.

And similarly, if you can't say 'gorblimey' in polite company nowadays, where can you say it?

The guidelines urge producers to refer any material they feel doubtful about to a higher authority and, where that's not possible, to 'err, if at all, on the side of caution'. In the immortal conclusion of the booklet: ' "When in doubt take it out" is the wisest maxim.'

When in doubt take it out? Now, I could add a joke here, in the form of a heartfelt endorsement for that indisputably wise maxim. However, I am aware that there are issues of taste around such a joke, and, seeing as Daphne the under-housemaid has finally departed for the stable block and I seem to be presently alone at my desk here, with nobody of higher authority to refer to, I am erring on the side of caution and omitting that joke altogether.

When in doubt take it out: you know it makes sense.

It's also fascinating to see how, back in 1948, there were strict proscriptions in place regarding impersonations, too.

'Certain artists,' my trusty volume of regulations tells us, 'have informed the Corporation that no unauthorised impersonations may be broadcast.'

And who were the artists with the authority to declare themselves an impression-free zone without prior permission in 1948? Well, the document names them, which is why I'm able to inform you that, back then, your impersonation of Gracie Fields, no matter how uncanny it was, would not have been welcome on the airwaves of the BBC unless Gracie herself had given you the nod.

And nor, equally, would your impression of Vera Lynn. Both those legendary wartime entertainers are specifically declared by the booklet to be out of bounds, except in special circumstances, for any forties-era Rory Bremner who fancies having a go.

Which says an enormous amount, clearly, about the standing of Gracie Fields and Vera Lynn in the country at that time. Talk about the nation's favourites. These days not even Tess Daly and Claudia Winkleman have that much clout.

Now, imagine the poor comedy scriptwriter in 1948, reading all this and thinking, 'Rats! So much for my skit in which a hotel chambermaid enters the room of a honeymoon couple with a Hoover and does a Vera Lynn impression on the way out. Some of my best material, too!'

Noise of paper being crumpled up and lobbed towards the bin.

However, as amusingly fussy as they now seem to us, maybe those 1948 BBC restrictions had something going for them. After all, they didn't stop the Goons from happening. They didn't stop Peter Ustinov or Kenneth Williams from happening either. They didn't stop that golden age of radio comedy that we were talking about in the previous chapter. Those rules forced the writers to be imaginative in order to get around them. Those tight, almost suffocating restrictions were a challenge to rise to, and maybe some of the biggest laughs in that era lay in bending those rules as far as they would go without breaking them.

It was the same, years later, for John Sullivan with *Only Fools*. Of course the rules were different – but there were still rules. Rules on swearing, for instance, which was entirely out of bounds for a prime-time comedy show.

But those were rules which simply forced John to be inventive. You wanted to see Del get frustrated and start throwing some choice language around, because you knew that was his likely response. But there was no choice language you were allowed to use.

So, what if you gave Del the habit of coming out with snatches of French which he didn't really understand – phrases that he'd picked up and liked the sound of because he thought they made him sound sophisticated? And what if occasionally he would reach for one of those French phrases to express his exasperation?

In short, what if, in a moment of irritation, at a point where he would be most likely to swear, he cried out 'Chateauneuf du Pape!'

That's genius, for me – the perfect example of the rule-swerve. It's funny, irrespective of whether you know that Del's actually just shouted something off the label of a wine bottle. And suddenly you've got swearing in the programme without having swearing in the programme.

I would definitely argue that having Del shout out something stupid in French was much funnier than having Del come out with something unmistakably Anglo-Saxon. And maybe that's a bit of a problem for comedy now. In a world where the rules are no longer so strict about swearing, people go straight for the unmistakably Anglo-Saxon. And that's less clever, and ultimately less funny.

Or to put it another way: you're better off in the long term calling someone a plonker.

* * *

Another breakfast, another set of morning newspapers – and another story about *Only Fools*.

'Strobes,' I say, looking across in a state of puzzlement to where the trusty retainer is deftly completing the 'milk art' in the froth of my cappuccino. 'Have Nick Lyndhurst and I had a falling-out?'

'No, sir,' says Strobes, expertly using two drips of espresso to finish the ears on a remarkably lifelike representation of a panda. 'That would not be possible, sir.'

'Then why does it say so here in the *Daily Bugle*?'*

'I can only suggest, sir,' says Strobes, 'that the papers are up to their old mischief again.'

Well, it's certainly not the first time that this story of a bust-up between me and Nick has made it into print. And it's not the first time it's had me scratching my head and thinking, 'Where did *that* come from?'

What tends to happen is this. One of us will be asked an innocent-sounding question about whether our *Only Fools* partnership is ever coming back to the screen. And we'll answer that, sadly, no it isn't, because John Sullivan is no longer with us, not since 2011, and without John there can't really be any more *Only Fools*.

And before you know it, that exchange will have generated the story: 'I'll never work with David Jason/Nicholas Lyndhurst again, says Nicholas Lyndhurst/David Jason.'

* Actual name of newspaper redacted to spare blushes.

And then all of a sudden there's a feud going on. Papers do seem to love a feud. 'Feud, glorious feud,' as they sing in *Oliver!* and also, it would appear, in the offices of various tabloids.

Similarly, if I'm asked whether Nick and I see each other a lot these days, and I say 'Not as much as we'd like to', I can't simply be saying that we wish we had more opportunities to get together, which is the case. I have to be implying that there has been a 'cooling off' in our relationship.

And nor can Nick and I can ever just be 'getting on with our lives' or 'going about our separate businesses', because that wouldn't be any kind of story at all. We always have to have 'grown apart'.

Now, I'm well aware that, in the larger scheme of things, none of this stuff really matters all that much. But it is a bit frustrating to see it out there, this story of a rift between Nick and me, especially what with it being so untrue. And I'm not sure, really, why the pair of us should attract it. Maybe it's some kind of hangover or confusion arising from all the lines that Del genuinely did throw Rodney's way in the series.

'You look like a blood donor who couldn't say no.'

'Sit down, Rodney, and keep your brains warm.'

Or this priceless exchange, which I really loved:

Rodney: 'Del, I've been thinking . . .'

Del: 'Oh, leave it out, Rodney, we're in enough trouble as it is.'

Or maybe it's one of the stranger consequences of having played a couple of brothers in a very popular comedy show. People detect that Nick and I aren't in and out of our Peckham flat quite so much these days and wonder what's up.

'You never see them sitting in armchairs and bickering any more, the way they did when they were on the telly,' some people connected with newspapers seem to say. 'Has something gone wrong between them, do you suppose?'

But there's nothing to see here. You're a pair of actors, brought together by a television show. You work wonderfully well together, and some golden moments ensue. You also rub along famously when the cameras aren't rolling and have a lot of laughs together. I mean, seriously: *loads* of laughs.

Yet of course the show ends. The circus moves on. You do other jobs. You have your own families and friends, your own sets of circumstances, just like you did before you met. You see each other very happily when the time allows – but so often the time simply *doesn't* allow.

In short, you're not getting together every night in the Nag's Head to shoot the breeze, much as people would maybe like to imagine you are. The show becomes a memory for you, too. A truly indelible memory, in the case of *Only Fools*. But a memory, nonetheless.

And that's not just Nick and me and *Only Fools*. That's how it happens all over. Although thinking about it, no other show that I've done, or acting partnership that I've

been in, seems to attract this sort of story. For example, Pam
Ferris and I aren't in each other's company nearly so much
nowadays as we were when we were filming *The Darling Buds
of May*. But I've yet to open the *Daily Bugle* and see anyone
wondering what *we* must have fallen out over.

And we weren't merely siblings in that show, we were actually married! Wait until the papers get hold of that one . . .*

With Nick, I feel slightly to blame for some of this fake
'feud' news, because what's often used as supporting evidence in these stories is a tale I told in an earlier volume of
these memoirs, about Nick and me having an enormous fight
during a location shoot for *Only Fools*.

And we did have a huge row that day – a truly spectacular
one. The kind of all-out, shouting, swearing, object-throwing
barney that relationships don't often come back from.

The only thing being, it was a play-fight – a wind-up, a
practical joke we played on the rest of the cast and crew.

It was raining, the cameras hadn't turned over all
morning – it was one of those frustrating days. Nick and
I had already exhausted the wide variety of entertainment
opportunities available to us at such times – which is to say,
we'd read the papers and then we'd used those papers to have

* Pam played Ma Larkin to my Pa Larkin in those lovely series we made
between 1991 and 1993. Along with Phillip Franks, who was Charlie
the tax inspector, we went back to the farm in Kent where the show was
shot, to film a reunion in 2017. Perhaps that public sighting has kept
the press off our case.

a paper-plane-building competition and seen who could fly their plane furthest.*

We were bored stiff, frankly, and the devil famously makes work for idle actors . . .

The pair of us were seated in the deluxe trailer that the BBC automatically provided in those days for its talent on location shoots – in fact a small, nicotine-stained caravan with some disturbingly grubby soft furnishings which possibly dated back to the sixties, and certainly hadn't been washed since then.

In this, our alluring home-from-home, we were basically drumming our fingers and chatting distractedly to pass the time. And at one point I started telling Nick about something I had got up to one time on a building site, years before all this.

Equally bored one day, while ostensibly employed to do the wiring in a new block of flats, me and my fellow spark Johnny Dingle had cooked up a bright scheme to stage a mock fight – abuse, fisticuffs, tools hurled out the window, the works. The plan was to convince the builders, working down below, that it really was kicking off between us, all for the pleasure of seeing their concerned faces as they ran up to find out what was happening.

---

* It's my book, so I'm going to say I won. But it was most likely Nick. He was exceptionally good at building paper planes. If it had been an Olympic sport he would never have had to take up acting.

As I related this tale, I saw a gleam come into Nick's eye. We could do that! We could stage a flaming row, convince everyone on the set that we'd had a massive falling-out . . .

Now, what I should perhaps have mentioned to Nick at that point was that my and Johnny's scrap had gone down really badly. Hearing the noise, the builders had come running up, just as we'd hoped.

'Gotcha!' we'd said. 'Not really fighting! Just pretending!'

And the whole thing had turned to dust. We thought they would see the funny side and find it all marvellously amusing. In fact, they had just charged up three flights of steps for no reason and were furious with us for wasting their time and energy.

Indeed, up to that point Johnny and I had been very welcome to join those builders over break times in a garage downstairs, where they had the precious facility to make a brew. We lost our invitation to tea for a couple of days after that until the cloud of resentment blew over.

Mind you, the tea was made in a bucket over a burner, into which you dipped your mug, like a ladle, and it was arguably the worst cup of tea you'd ever tasted, so maybe it was a small price to pay.

Anyway, somehow the detail of the original prank's flat outcome slipped my mind, and Nick and I duly went ahead with our 'fight'. We did some careful planning and then, at the appointed moment, when the queue for the food wagon adjacent to our caravan had become long enough to constitute a decent audience, we executed it.

We did some shouting at first, which slowly escalated, followed by some thumps from within the caravan, as of furniture going over. And then Nick – really throwing himself into the role with a vengeance, I felt – burst out of the caravan and set off into the distance, all hunched over in fury, while I stood at the door and bawled after him that that was it, the absolute limit, that our working relationship was over, and that he should never darken my towels again.

Then I went and sat in the caravan, pretending to be simmering with rage and hurt, while Nick went and sat somewhere else and did likewise.

Naturally this explosive scene caused consternation among the watching crew, who were curious about what, exactly, had made things go so badly pear-shaped between us, and who were also anxious about what this spelt for the rest of the day's shoot, and indeed the future of the series.

Delegations came to us individually to see if they could find out what the problem was, but Nick and I sullenly refused their diplomacy. Eventually somebody went off and summoned the producer to come and see if he could work his personal magic, at which point Nick and I realised we had probably pushed it as far as we could. Especially as the producer wasn't on set at this point and had to travel in specially.

So we did our big reveal.

And again, exactly as on the building site, the 'gotcha' moment went down like a cup of cold sick. People were more annoyed than amused.

'We were only having a laugh!'

'But we didn't know that.'

'Well, you weren't supposed to.'

I guess it passed a lunch hour. But that episode does, at least, tell you something about my and Nick's relationship, which you might bear in mind the next time the 'feud' story circulates. The only way we could find something to fall out over was by inventing it. And that's still true.

Funnily enough, for all this talk of slow days, my abiding memory of those *Only Fools* shoots is of being in a frantic hurry. We were always in a rush to get things done, working hard against the clock. It was especially the case when the episodes went from thirty minutes to fifty minutes, without any extension of the shooting time – a very BBC move, that. 'Yes, your show can have the extra length you've been begging for, but you've still got exactly the same amount of time in which to make it.' For a short while we were turning in six-day weeks on location, and then rushing into the studio for the Sunday shoot in front of the audience practically out of breath.

Thankfully, that relaxed a little eventually, and we started getting ten days for each episode. But even then the schedules were still tight. Tony Dow, the director, could get a bit shirty with us sometimes for needing so many takes because we were cracking up. But then fair enough, because, as the precious seconds ticked by, he could see his shooting schedule disappearing up the spout, so he had to be a bit stern about it.

I suppose one solution would have been to make the show less funny, but I'm not sure anyone was really interested in talking to John Sullivan about that.

One of the reasons I think Nick and I blended together so well is that we shared the same attitude to being up against a deadline, as we so often were. We both complained about it quite a lot, but we also both rather relished it. The shortness of the time available to us, the fact that we always seemed to be in an almighty scrap with the ticking of the clock, ignited something in us.

It's tempting sometimes to think that things would be better if only you had more time. But that's not always the case. More time is a nice luxury, but it doesn't necessarily mean better work. Sometimes the work you do when the pressure is really on turns out to be your best. That was true of *Only Fools* where time always seemed to be at a premium and the ethos was generally 'Have that ready by yesterday afternoon, please'. Very often the rush gave the show its energy, its momentum. You can see it in our eyes sometimes. We're fired up. We're right at it.

Still, we did get time to breathe every now and then. The problem, after a while, was knowing what to do with that time. Once the show got popular you would often find yourself slightly hemmed in on set by people coming to have a look and catch a glimpse of you. None of us had really known levels of recognition quite like it before, so it took some getting used to.

For me and Nick it reached the stage on the location shoots where if we wanted to go out at lunchtime, or go for a walk and stretch our legs without getting stopped along the way, we needed to cover up. I would stick on a porkpie hat and some sunglasses. Nick might go for sunglasses and a baseball cap.

I know: what superlative masters of disguise the pair of us were.

The thing is, it worked. Indeed, it worked extremely well. And exactly how well it worked we discovered the day we both went out separately onto the streets of Bristol for a wander.

I remember walking by this bloke in sunglasses and a baseball cap and getting a bit further along the road before I thought, 'Hang on a minute, wasn't that . . . ?'

And meanwhile Nick was walking in the other direction and thinking, 'Hang on a sec, that bloke in the porkpie hat looked a bit familiar . . .'

And then, at almost exactly the same time, we both turned round, amid the sound of two pennies loudly dropping.

'It's you!'

Life was rather imitating art there.

I sometimes like to think of Del and Rodney as a south

London Laurel and Hardy. Nick could do a really good Stan Laurel impression, actually – the hapless smile, the fingers dopily scratching the top of the head. Both of us were fans. The films Laurel and Hardy made with the Hal Roach studio are unsurpassed in comedy, in my opinion. I cannot imagine ever watching *The Music Box* and not finding it funny. It seems to me to contain some magical comic essence which is utterly timeless.

And there were plenty of scenarios in *Only Fools* in which Del might reasonably have turned to Rodney, or vice versa, and said: 'Well, here's another nice mess you've gotten me into.'* There's a similar, if more understated, physical comedy going on, too: the little bloke and the bigger bloke. And there's a similar emotional chemistry too. Like Stan and Ollie, Del and Rodney would get irritated with each other but they also had an unbreakable bond, and that bond would always survive.

The chandelier scene, for example, is pure Stan and Ollie, with that long, slow look at each other after the precious

---

* It's frequently misquoted, that line. People tend to say, 'Well, that's another fine mess you've gotten us into.' But *Another Fine Mess* was the title of one of Laurel and Hardy's films, from 1930, and Hardy will far more commonly accuse Laurel of getting him into 'another nice mess'. Also, according to one film buff's calculations, Hardy's most frequently used catchphrase has nothing to do with messes: it's 'Why don't you do something to help me?' He repeats that line more than any other. Very happy to clear all that up.

object comes crashing down, in dawning horror at what has just occurred.

John Sullivan had told me that story one night in the BBC bar. It was a tale about his dad, who confidently took on odd jobs to make ends meet, irrespective of whether he had any previous experience in the field, and who once accordingly found himself cleaning a pair of chandeliers at a country house somewhere.

And apparently John's dad and his mate had stood with a blanket underneath one of the chandeliers, waiting to catch it when it was unbolted from the floor above, and . . . well, you know what happened next. They had solemnly watched one of the room's other chandeliers come crashing to the ground.

I thought this was one of the funniest professional mishaps I'd ever heard of. The wonderful overestimation of their own talents and the classic slapstick disaster that resulted – it was . . . well, Laurel and Hardy-esque. It was *The Music Box* in another form, really. And I was absolutely adamant. 'John, you've just got to write that. It's too good.'

And so it was that Nick and I duly found ourselves up a pair of ladders and shooting the most highly pressured scene in the whole of the making of *Only Fools*. Pretty much all of the big set pieces on that show involved multiple takes. Sometimes that was just to try different approaches that might work better. And sometimes it was simply while we all got the laughter out of our systems.

But that wasn't going to wash this time. This was a one-take moment. It was made very clear to us that there was only the one chandelier available for this stunt and that it cost £6,000, which the budget department had not been separated from lightly.

Not so much as the tiniest flicker of amusement was to cross Nick's and my faces when that expensive prop smashed because if either of us looked anything other than mortified at this moment the whole gag was lost, with no going back. Ray Butt, the director, was so stern about the consequences of us screwing this up that Nick actually thought his job was on the line and the series along with it.

A Herculean effort of seriousness was required, then – which we were perhaps not famous for. But we dug deep and kept our faces straight. After the chandelier dropped, we gave it ten seconds of silence for safety with Nick and me staring at each other, while out of the corner of our eyes we could both see Ray Butt – he who had laid it on the line to us so firmly – stuffing a handkerchief in his mouth in order to stifle his own laughter.

And then, finally, the golden word: 'Cut!'

I'm reminded of the remark from Mission Control in Houston when Neil Armstrong finally managed to touch down on the moon after a hair-raising search for a rock-free landing place.

'Houston, Tranquility Base here,' Armstrong said. 'The Eagle has landed.'

And from the ground came the relieved reply: 'Copy that, Tranquility. You got a bunch of guys about to turn blue. We're breathing again.'

We'd all been turning blue in those ten seconds and there was a massive exhalation of breath when it was all over. That was our Apollo 11 moment. The chandelier had landed.

All worth the effort, of course. It's one of those scenes that have come to define the show. Indeed, on the night *Only Fools* won its first BAFTA, that was the sequence screened before we went up to get the trophy.

We all managed to get on and off the stage without mishap that evening, which, given the high spirits and the fact that a certain amount of refreshment had been taken on board during the evening, was quite fortunate.

But alas, it was not always thus.

In 1997, the Batman and Robin sequence was up for Funniest Comedy Moment at the British Comedy Awards. Now I mention it, there's a trace of Stan and Ollie in that Batman and Robin scene, too – particularly in its ending, with the embarrassment of those two, obliged to mingle in their stupid costumes among the soberly dressed guests at a wake.

Anyway, neither Nick nor I could make it to the Comedy Awards that night, but Buster Merryfield, who played Uncle Albert, Gwyneth Strong, who played Cassandra, and Ken MacDonald, who played Mike the barman, went along to do the necessary.

Jonathan Ross was compering and the ridiculously

good-looking Sasha Distel was for some reason in charge of opening the envelope.

'And the award goes to . . . *Only Fools and Horses*.'

Up went the *Only Fools* party to receive their due, Buster enthusiastically leading the way.

I think a lot of people assumed at first that what happened next was a stunt – Buster simply entering into the spirit of the occasion on British comedy's big night, and producing some more British comedy, Uncle Albert-style, there and then, off the cuff.

But Buster tripped over just before reaching the steps at the side of the stage and went down with a right old thump. And there really wasn't anything funny about it from his point of view – it was a properly nasty fall. He banged his head on the edge of the steps, splitting the skin above his eye.

Much kerfuffle and consternation ensued. What was wrong with Buster? Had he tripped? Had he collapsed? How bad was the wound? All of this stuff had to be weighed in a hurry – and live on television, too. The cameras did that ominous thing they do when there's a bad injury in a football match – they pulled away to a discreet distance.

Eventually, though, the gang made it onto the stage – Buster bravely among them, with a bloodied head, the extent of the damage now visible – and the prize was handed over, albeit still rather anxiously and with an understandably muted atmosphere in the room.

'Comedy's a tough business,' said Ken, making what must

have been one of the briefest acceptance speeches an awards night has ever seen.

'A tough business,' confirmed Buster.

And then he was quickly ushered off to be patched up.

Honestly, I let these people out of my sight for five minutes, and look what happens.

But all credit to Buster, bless his memory, for getting back on his feet, deciding it was only a flesh wound, getting up on that stage and obeying to the letter the age-old theatrical maxim: the awards show must go on.

All mishaps and physical damage aside, I loved the idea of an *Only Fools* sequence receiving an award, and that award being picked up on the night by cast members who weren't in that particular scene. It firmly underscores the fact these shows are a team game where everyone depends on everyone else.

And here's an example of what I mean by that. There's another sequence from *Only Fools*, probably repeated even more frequently than the Batman and Robin one, and the chandelier one, in which Del goes out with Trigger to a wine bar and is just starting to fancy his chances with a girl across the room when, wine glass in hand, he leans to the side and . . .

OK, maybe you know this sequence.

And people might refer to it as 'the moment when Del falls through the bar flap'. But think about how much is going on around that fall of mine that makes the scene work the way it does. Think how much more that scene amounts to than just a shot of one bloke going over.

Think, for example, how differently the scene would play if the member of the bar staff who emerges from behind the bar and fatally lifts the flap, while Del and Trigger are talking, didn't do it at speed and in one fluid, unobtrusive movement so that you register it, yet without really thinking anything of it.

Then consider the camera angle and the choice of a mid-shot which draws no particular attention to the bar flap at all. Think of the many ways in which it might have been tempting to signal the raising of the bar flap far more strongly – and consider what a good idea it was NOT to do that.

All of these tiny decisions were taken, over and around decisions about the nature of the fall itself. And all of them were crucial to the ultimate effect.

And how differently the scene would play without Trigger standing there – Trigger in his electric-blue suit. You need Del, in his raincoat, to be tucked in beside Trigger there, the two of them already presenting a ticklishly comic spectacle even before the fall happens.

And, yes, I'm proud of the clean lines of that fall – of dropping to one side without instinctively putting my hand out to stop myself, which brings another comic dimension to it, and is quite hard to do, I don't mind saying. All those years of bruising myself in farces up and down the country were not in vain.

But it's Trigger gormlessly looking away as Del goes over sideways that accentuates the fall's ridiculousness and accelerates the humour of the moment. It means that, for the audience, the fall comes with a double punch: we get to laugh at Del falling over and we get to laugh at Trigger not seeing him go. We're in on the moment and out on the edge of it at the same time.

And, as he turns through 180 degrees and starts scanning the bar all the way across to the door, it's Trigger's particularly Trigger-like puzzlement about Del's sudden disappearance that clinches the scene. Had it been – to put it delicately – a sharper member of the ensemble (had it been Boycie, say, or Mike), the double take at that point would have played differently. But it's Trigger, and we know what Trigger is like, so that incomprehension about Del vanishing into thin air has its own lovely weight.

And consider the difference if you cut the scene there, on Trigger's bafflement. It might have seemed a plausible enough moment to end it – to go out on the big laugh. And it would have meant I could have crawled away off the crash mat and straight away begun the important work of nursing my bruises.

But you need the aftermath. You need Del scrambling back to his feet. You need Trigger completing the full 360 degrees and giving a little start upon finding Del suddenly next to him again. You need Del flexing his neck, making like it never happened. You need those moments for the audience's laughter to continue washing through, because, as you learn in the theatre, laughter as strong as that is not the kind you want to be cutting off in order to move on. It's too precious and, having earned it, you want to give that laughter some space to indulge itself.

But you need those recovery moments, too, to underscore the rubber nature of Del's spirit, which we talked about earlier. Life has once more contrived to put him on the floor, but there he is again, look – bouncing back, at least a little way, and we're with him when he does so.

And that, too, is straight out of Laurel and Hardy, and those moments where the pair of them, after some ridiculous slapstick upset or set-to, get a moment to set their bowler hats back on and straighten their ties and carry on up the road. Del, as always at these lowest ebbs, gets a chance at least partially to restore his dignity and put himself in a position to come back for more. Because, yes, we laugh at Del, but we're on his side as well. It's what gives these moments their humanity.

So, yes – a team game. And what a team. I'm looking at a photo which Carol Challis, John's widow, recently turned up. It's a still from 'The Jolly Boys' Outing' special, taken somewhere in Margate in the summer of 1989: Nick, me, Buster, John, Roger and Ken, plus a stupid inflatable dolphin, all in a line with arms linked and laughing our heads off. Even the inflatable dolphin seems to be in on the joke, by the looks of things. Or he's certainly smiling about something.

145

There's nothing special about the picture: it's actually rather blurry and our feet are cut off, in the classic 'holiday snapshot' style. No matter. Maybe partly *because* of that 'family album' feel to the picture, it takes me all the way back there, it really does.

Thirty-five years ago – half a lifetime.

And as I'm looking at it, here's the thing that comes up and bites me: Nick and I are the only two of that group that are still around. Ken, Buster, Roger, John – they've all left us in the meantime. Lennard, too, before any of them. All these great performers, all these great colleagues of mine – all gone. Just me and Nick left standing, from that brave band of utterly loveable fools.

So if you ever see a story in the papers saying that Nick and I are 'feuding', after all we did together, and with the past we share . . . well, you know what to think of it.

CHAPTER FOUR

Of gunfire, bomb sites and Beatles managers

Once upon a time, an eight-year-old girl was taken along by her parents to watch her older brother play King Duncan in a production of Shakespeare's *Macbeth*.

Duncan's first appearance is in the second scene of that play, when a wounded soldier arrives, just off the battlefield. And this little girl's brother, as Duncan, standing on the stage, duly looked at this bedraggled and wounded figure and spoke his first line:

'What bloody man is that?'

The little girl couldn't believe her ears: her brother had just said 'bloody'! Bold as you like! And he'd only just come onstage!

In that split second the girl realised something important about acting which she hadn't previously understood and which seemed to her deeply appealing: it was a licence to swear in front of your parents.

Who wouldn't want to be an actor in that case? And just

147

like that, the future course of Judi Dench (for it was she) was set and the rest, as they say, is history, a damehood and a series of extremely enviable appearances in James Bond movies.

So now I ponder: what, for me, was the obscure germinal moment from which all followed? What was the seed that, once planted in my young and innocent mind, would later, as with Judi, bloom into a life in acting and a damehood – or at least the nearest male equivalent?

Of course, unlike Judi, my planted seed wouldn't lead to me getting asked to play M in any James Bond movies. But you can't have everything. And if anyone asks, I'm still working on that. Although I'm mainly holding out for the role of Bond, obviously. It's time they went for a slightly older actor there, isn't it? Someone with a few miles on the clock and some proper range and depth of acting experience behind him. Just saying.*

So, what was it that first whispered to my childish mind that acting might have something going for it? I'm spinning

---

* If you will permit me a name-drop here, Dame Judi and I were seated next to each other at a charity dinner organised by *The Repair Shop's* Jay Blades not so long ago – our first ever meeting. And what a laugh that was – we got on like a house on fire. We agreed that acting was a serious business, but, at the end of the day, not THAT serious, and if you weren't having fun while you were doing it, you were probably doing it wrong. Someone after my own heart there, definitely. Still no word on that Bond role though, sadly, but I'm sure she's pulling the strings on my behalf as hard as she possibly can, even as we speak.

back through the deepest recesses of my memory here. I don't think it was spotting the chance to swear in the hearing of my mum and dad, as thrilling as that might have seemed. (Swearing was strictly forbidden at home.) If anything, it was probably sensing the chance of getting properly involved in a gunfight – and ideally from the back of a charging horse.

And it definitely wasn't at a school production of Macbeth – gunfire and horses generally being in short supply at those. It was in the cinema watching John Wayne.

Seen from a seat in the stalls, in the company of my mother, on a Tuesday or a Thursday evening – and sometimes both – those great Wayne westerns made an enormous impression on my childhood mind.

Looking back, though, my career has offered me disappointingly few opportunities to wield guns in the way my boyhood self might have felt inspired by. Almost none, in fact.

There was Del's moment with a borrowed shotgun at the clay pigeon shoot in 'A Royal Flush', of course. Does that count?

And actually, Del turned out to have a positively Wayne-like accuracy in his shooting on that occasion, to the amazement of everybody watching – another of those neat John Sullivan comic twists, running directly counter to the more obvious and possibly expected comedy of Del proving to be an utterly hopeless shot, and thereby getting a bigger laugh as a consequence. So, perhaps to that extent this scene represented the fulfilment of that childhood dream.

On the other hand, Del departed the scene in a yellow Robin Reliant, which rather deflated the glamour of the moment.

Just about the only other time I can think of where a character I was playing was required to handle a gun in earnest was in *March in the Windy City*. That was a TV movie for ITV that the producer David Reynolds put me up for, soon after *The Darling Buds of May*, when I was looking for something in a more serious vein.

That hunt would eventually lead me to *A Touch of Frost*, but in the meantime there was this thriller – filmed on location in Chicago, don't you know. Well, *some* of it was. The rest of it was shot in Yorkshire. And my character, March, carried a gun. In a holster, what's more. So at one point I found myself creeping quietly along a hotel corridor, hearing voices coming from the other side of a door, and reaching into the holster for my gun.

To be perfectly honest with you, that's the only bit of the film I now recall – one brief moment in a hotel corridor. And I fear it may be more than most viewers remember.

Incidentally, did you know that John Wayne once watched an episode of *It Ain't Half Hot Mum*?

I know – for some reason it's almost as hard to imagine John Wayne sitting down to watch *It Ain't Half Hot Mum* as it is to imagine him acting in it.

But apparently it's true: he found himself parked in front of the show at some point in 1974 when he was filming in the UK and staying at a hotel in London.

And his verdict? Well, it was a big thumbs down from the Duke, apparently. He was not dazzled.

Well, he would have his reasons, I'm sure. There may have been some cultural barriers there which prevented the programme from fully landing with an American. Also, I guess if you've been in *Sands of Iwo Jima*, the prospect of a noisy Welsh sergeant major ticking off 'La-Di-Dah' Gunner Graham during rehearsals for a piano-led musical number might not impress you all that much by way of on-screen spectacle.

But wait a minute, because it seems John Wayne did like *one* thing about the show. As whichever episode it was unfolded before his weary eyes, the star of *True Grit* is alleged to have sighed and said, 'Well, at least the guy playing the sergeant major has a great voice.'

Did word of this approval ever filter through to Windsor Davies, the owner of that great voice and the actor who played the aforementioned bawling Welsh sergeant major? I sincerely hope so. Imagine getting praise from the mighty John Wayne!

And imagine getting praise from the mighty John Wayne and never knowing about it!

Given my feelings about Wayne, I would probably have overcome all the scepticism I spoke of earlier about retirement and, with an elegant bow, withdrawn from the business forever on the strength of that single endorsement alone.*

Now, much as John Wayne was disappointed by *It Ain't Half Hot Mum*, so my dad was downcast, to say the least, to hear his son's early dreams and inspirations had finally solidified and he was quitting his job as an electrician to forge a whole new career in the theatre. And in fairness to my dad, it's hard to see how he could have felt otherwise.

My father had started working life as a fish porter at Billingsgate, getting up before dawn every morning and cycling about twelve miles to the market to cart wet fish about. Then he'd taken a job as a fishmonger at Mac Fisheries in Camden where he spent the rest of his working days wading around in rubber boots on a cold, slippery floor – work which would ultimately earn him a crippling dose of arthritis in his legs and feet for his retirement. (In his final years, my dad needed two sticks to get anywhere and was practically chair-bound.)

---

* Actually, I've just thought about that a bit harder, and I wouldn't. But I certainly would have been delighted with it – absolutely made up. Wayne, who died in 1979, wasn't sure about television. 'I don't know whether I love it or hate it,' he once said. 'But there sure has never been any form of entertainment so available to the human race with so little effort since they invented marital sex.' Plenty to think about there. I can only imagine he said this on a different day from the one on which he watched *It Ain't Half Hot Mum*. Incidentally, several years before he first shouted 'Shut up!' at 'La-Di-Dah' Gunner Graham, Windsor was in a production of *Under Milk Wood* with me. We'll have very good cause to mention this production later on.

But that was work as my dad understood it. And acting didn't really come anywhere near it. My job as an electrician was steady and reliable – the kind of employment that would see you out. People were always going to need electricians, weren't they?

But acting? No guarantees there, were there? And I mean, not wishing to be rude or anything, but . . . was that even work? Not from where my dad was sitting. It was nothing he was ever likely to relate to.

My family was, I have come to realise, raised within a certain set of beliefs about what it was to be British and working class – beliefs that were entirely common then and still hold some sway today. You had a very strong sense that your position in life and the range of your ambition, such as it was, had been allotted to you at birth, and that you had no business reaching beyond that or trying to imagine your life some other way.

You felt it at school, definitely, where there seemed to be a willingness to educate you, but not *too* much. And you felt it at home, too – the idea that an unalterable course had been set for you, irrespective of any talents or ambitions you might have. 'The likes of us' was a phrase I heard a lot in my childhood. There were things that were for the likes of us, and there were things that were not for the likes of us. Being an actor was definitely one of the things not for the likes of us.

I had actually discussed with my parents the possibility of

taking up acting a few years before this. The conversation hadn't gone well.

I was about seventeen or eighteen at the time, and I forget now exactly which stage I was at. I was either working in the car repair garage, which was my very first job, or at the start of my apprenticeship with the Electricity Board, which was what I next signed up for. But I had also been acting for a couple of years with the Incognito Group. And one of our productions had just been entered in a festival and done well, and there was a little reception for us afterwards at Friern Barnet Town Hall.

I recall that tea and biscuits were served, and I recall, too, the excruciating feeling of having no idea how to behave in this kind of mix-and-mingle social situation, which seemed very posh to me and like nothing I was prepared for.

As I stood there awkwardly holding my teacup on its saucer, a woman approached me. She had glasses and looked a lot like one of my schoolteachers, which probably put me on the back foot a bit. But she was from the council, in fact, and very friendly, and very complimentary about my acting which she had just seen.

She asked me, 'Have you ever thought about becoming an actor, professionally?'

I shook my head and said no. I think I would have felt embarrassed to tell her anything else.

She said, 'Have you ever thought about going to drama school?'

Again, I told her it wasn't something I had ever considered – which I certainly hadn't.

She then said, 'Well, if you do ever think about it, I think the council would be persuaded to support you.'

There were grants available, it seemed. This councillor was telling me that if I wanted to study drama she had the wherewithal to make it possible and get the tuition fees covered.

Well, here was a thought. It might not have been something that had occurred to me before, but by the time I got home that evening I had become extremely excited about the idea. Give acting a proper shot? Go to college on some kind of scholarship? Why not?

I thought my parents might be excited about it, too. But I was gravely mistaken there. I'd barely finished getting the words out before my father said, 'Well, you won't be able to live *here*, then.'

They simply weren't in the position to contemplate supporting a student, living at home, for however long it was going to take. They were struggling and they couldn't stretch to it. That was the verdict and the discussion ended there.

So that was my little balloon thoroughly deflated.

I could hardly complain, though. It was just economics, plain and simple. As things stood, I was earning. I was bringing in my 'keep', handing it over to my mother on a Friday from my pay packet: thirty shillings, as I remember, from my three pounds a week. And that was how it had to stay until I was earning enough to be out of the house altogether.

Of course, it worked out OK in the end. I got to do the job that I really wanted to do. And I got to do it at a point when I really knew how badly I wanted to do it. Would a stint at drama school have made any difference to me? I might have got on a bit quicker, possibly, but even that wasn't guaranteed. But I got there my own way, learning on the job, and maybe the lessons I learned taking that route were more valuable to me in the long run.

So, no, I didn't have formal training. But at the same time I can't really consider myself self-taught because I had so many great teachers: Ronnie Barker, especially, but Bob Monkhouse, too, and Ron Moody, and, in fact, every actor that I worked alongside who took the trouble to talk to me about things and share some of what they knew. I never shied away from asking people for advice and I never stopped learning from them and pushing myself to learn more. I had a very privileged education in that respect.

It must have steadied some of my dad's nerves and allayed his worst fears about the perils of the acting trade to see his son eventually, after a stuttering start, getting work in the theatre and parts on television. He wasn't around to see me get knighted which I've always felt sad about. I would have loved to have taken him to Buckingham Palace for the ceremony, have him watch the Queen wield the sword. That would have been a seal of approval which he would really have understood. Pride didn't come easily to him, but that would have made him proud, definitely.

Though I reckon he still wouldn't have thought that what I did was proper work.

And you know what? Compared with what he did, he'd have had a point.

*　　*　　*

The story goes that when Princess Margaret was introduced to Brian Matthew, she said to him, perhaps a bit sniffily, 'You started all this *DJ lark*, didn't you?'

Well, I don't know whether anyone needed to be sniffy about it, but Her Royal Highness was definitely on to something there. Brian *did* sort of start all that disc jockey lark. At any rate, in the sixties his rich, rounded tones were all over the airwaves. He had pop music shows on BBC Radio, when those things were few and far between, and a show on Radio Luxembourg.

And he was on ITV, presenting *Thank Your Lucky Stars*, which always sounded like it should have been a game show but which was in fact a kind of prototype *Top of the Pops* where bands came on and mimed to their hits, and which included a slot where the latest releases were reviewed. All the big sixties pop acts, from the Beatles and the Rolling Stones downwards, appeared on *Thank Your Lucky Stars*, and Brian was the man welcoming them aboard.

Eventually Brian moved to Radio 2, presenting shows like *Round Midnight* and *Sounds of the Sixties*. By the time he died, in 2017 at the age of eighty-eight, he had been presenting at the BBC for sixty-three years.

So, in the mid-sixties, Brian was right at the beating heart of the new pop scene, gaining him considerable glamour by association.

Which made it quite thrilling, then, and also more than a little surprising, that a certain 25-year-old electrician from Finchley occasionally found himself entertained by Brian and his wife Pamela at their very nice house in south-east London, and splashing about in their swimming pool.

And no, I wasn't there to do the electrics, though I can understand your logic.

The thing was, Brian and Pamela were friends of a friend of mine, Simon Oates, and, what with me being a keen am-dram actor, Simon thought I ought to meet Brian and Pamela, for reasons which will become apparent. So I tagged along with Simon to a couple of parties that Brian and Pamela threw at their home, which sat at the very edge of the city, just where everything turns green and starts being Kent instead.

I have memories of a large and comfortable detached house on a hill, and of larking about on the low, springy diving board beside the pool in this house's extensive garden and thinking, 'Well, *this* is all right.'

And then I would chat to Brian, who could tell you tales of

THIS TIME NEXT YEAR

travelling with the Beatles on their 1964 tour of America, or of being the announcer for *Hancock's Half Hour* in the 1950s, and how Tony Hancock would come in every week and, still in his hat and coat, sit and thumb through that week's script, muttering and tutting about how awful it was – which, of course, invariably it wasn't, or certainly not once Hancock had finished delivering it.

The thing about Brian that tended to go under the wire a bit was that he loved acting. That was probably his greatest enthusiasm, in fact, over and above the music. At one point in his life he must have imagined that the theatre would be where his future lay. When his future turned out to be 'starting all this DJ lark', he carried on acting anyway, joining his local am-dram group, the Chelsfield Players.

Indeed, Brian and Pamela weren't just prominent in the Chelsfield Players, they seem to have ruled the company for a while. Brian directed almost every play the society put on in the eight years between 1958 and 1966, and the ones he didn't direct were directed by Pamela. In most cases, the two of them would play the leading roles as well.

However, not even that could sate Brian's passion for the boards. He had a theatre built onto his house on Chelsfield Hill – a neat little place with its own stage and auditorium. He called it the Pilgrim Little Theatre and he put on plays there.

Now, at this point in history I was still David White, and still about a month shy of getting my first professional engagement at the New Theatre in Bromley and changing my name in order to secure my Equity card.

But in the meantime, I was buzzing around and throwing myself into am-dram productions almost anywhere that anyone would have me – not just at the aforementioned Incogs but with other north London outfits as well, such as the Manor Players, where I would happily put myself out on loan if the diary would accommodate it. On account of that obsessiveness, Brian recognised in me something of a kindred spirit and he asked me to be in one of his Chelsfield Players productions.

Clearly it was slightly bonkers of me to commit to haring from one side of London to the other for rehearsals and then for the production itself, in a time when I was getting up early in the morning in Lodge Lane and going to work all day. But it was a chance to go onstage and act, so I said yes.

The play was Ben Travers's *Rookery Nook*, a twenties farce about a woman who turns up in pyjamas at a country house in the middle of the night claiming to be seeking refuge from her stepfather. Brian and Pamela both had roles, as did a certain David White, but over any further memories of that production, time seems to have drawn its trusty, fire-retardant safety curtain.

All I can tell you is what the little printed programme produced for the occasion tells me, which is that there was an interval for refreshments after Act One, and that the play ran for three consecutive nights in March 1965 – and was, no doubt, the talk of all Chelsfield for possibly minutes thereafter.

But that wasn't my only theatrical engagement with Brian Matthew. Around about this time, I also acted with him in a play he put on in his home theatre.

The Incognito Group had produced a piece called *The Dock Brief*, a clever little two-hander by John Mortimer. It's set in a prison cell where a lawyer turns up to prepare a felon's defence with him, only to reveal himself to be a bit of a bluffer. The felon keeps having to correct the lawyer on procedure and the relationship between the two eventually twists right round, until the felon is essentially representing the lawyer. It's really well constructed, and good fun to perform, and when Brian was looking for a play to put on, I mentioned it to him and he suggested we do it together.

I was once again the felon and Brian, in a curly wig, played the failing lawyer. And very good he was, too, by the way. Brian could seriously act. So we rehearsed this playlet and performed it a couple of times to packed and no doubt rapturous houses in that little auditorium.

I hadn't thought about all of that for quite a while. But then, partway into 2024, Brian and Pamela's god-daughter very thoughtfully wrote to Gill and me saying that she had come across a few photographs among Brian's papers, and also a letter, and asking if we'd be interested in having them. Naturally I said 'Yes, please', and shortly afterwards a couple of pictures arrived, including one of Brian and me acting together in *The Dock Brief*.

And along with those pictures came the letter.

It wasn't a letter to or from Brian, as it turned out; it was a letter that Brian had been copied in on: 'cc Brian Matthew' it said at the bottom. It was typewritten, on headed notepaper – NEMS Presentations Ltd – with an address in Argyle Street in London, dated September 1965, and directed to John Fernald at the Royal Academy of Dramatic Art, not far away in Gower Street.

'Dear John,' it began. 'My dear friend Brian Matthew (D.J.) has asked me to mention to you an actor called David Jason who he thinks of very highly.'

The writer then goes on to say that I will be appearing that week in a production of Sheridan's *The Rivals* at New Theatre, Bromley, where it urges the recipient to go and see me, adding, 'I assure you that I respect Brian's suggestions in this connection.'

Failing that, the writer suggests, Fernald could always offer this David Jason a brief audition in London and discover for himself how good he is.

The letter is signed 'Yours sincerely, Brian Epstein'.

At first, I couldn't believe what I was reading. Here was the manager of the Beatles, a man I had never met, urging the principal of RADA, another man I had never met, to have a look at my acting, and even perhaps to offer me a private audition.

And he was doing this at the point in my life when I had literally just started out in repertory theatre and was on the hunt for any break that I could get. And all at the instigation of Brian Matthew, who had never said anything about this to me, but, I now learned, had silently gone into battle on my behalf.

It's probably a good job Brian *didn't* mention it, actually, because the idea of someone coming up to me at that period in my life and saying 'Oh, by the way, I've asked the manager of the Beatles to put in a word for you' would most likely have caused me to fall flat on the floor and not get up for a month.

So, why did Brian Matthew ask Epstein to put in a word for me with John Fernald? I've been trying to work it out. Did he think that Fernald might want to open the door for me at RADA and usher me in to study at that august institution?

Well, it's possible. But what rather goes against that interpretation of the letter is the fact that 1965 is the year that Fernald had some kind of falling-out with RADA over its approach to things and decided to leave his job as principal, passing it on to Hugh Cruttwell, who took over at the end of that year and stayed in charge there until 1984. So even though the letter was sent to RADA, Fernald was officially on his way out the door at that point and recruiting new students was possibly the last thing on his mind.

Maybe, then, the letter relates to something else. Epstein knew Fernald because the Beatles' manager had been a

RADA student under him in the fifties. That doesn't seem to have worked out for Epstein, and he left after a couple of terms.

Now, though, with things in the pop music line going quite well for him, Epstein was in a position to produce plays. And in the week that Epstein sent this letter, a story appeared in the *Sunday Mirror* reporting that the Beatles' manager had signed Fernald to direct a play that Epstein was intending to put on in the West End – *A Smashing Day* by Alan Plater.

So maybe Epstein thought Fernald might want to have a look at me with a view to offering me a part in that. Either way, we're clearly looking here at one of those moments when, given a slightly stronger breeze and with the stars lined up in a slightly different order, things could have turned out completely differently for me.

For who, frankly, was more powerful in British entertainment at that point than the manager of the Beatles? I mean, as references go . . . The mighty voice of Brian Epstein had been raised on my behalf, and surely, at that moment in history, that was like having Caesar and his thumb on your case in the Colosseum during Roman times.

Think about it: this was September 1965. The Beatles had just released the movie *Help!* (Did I go and see it? Of course I did. It was pretty much the law that you went.) They were a month on from playing Shea Stadium in New York. And they were about to put out the *Rubber Soul* album. All of these cultural events are still enthusiastically talked about today.

And right in the middle of all this, here was their manager saying, 'Trust me, I heard it from Brian Matthew – that David Jason's all right.'

Epstein had serenely nodded in my direction, and surely people would now rush to enact his will. Either I was going to be plucked from the gutter to hone my thespian crafts among the silver-spooned elite at RADA, or I was going to go leapfrogging into a play in the West End, just a matter of mere weeks into my professional career.

But of course, my point here is that neither of these things came to pass. Nothing came of this potentially life-changing letter but silence, with perhaps the additional sound of tumbleweed bowling past the window. Almost sixty years of silence and tumbleweed, in fact. So completely did Fernald ignore the testimony of Mr Brian Epstein regarding my talents that I didn't get to hear about it until the other day.

Now, there could be any number of reasons why the soon-to-be-former principal of RADA ignored this hot tip from the man who brought the world the great gift of the Fab Four and, just for good measure (some might even say a bit of balance), Cilla Black, too. Maybe Epstein in those days was constantly shoving suggestions for actors Fernald's way, and he'd got a bit tired of it. Perhaps he was in the habit of carefully folding these letters up and, with a slow shake of his head, filing them under 'N' for 'no thanks' in his waste bin.

Or maybe Fernald *did* consider coming to have a look at me in *The Rivals*, but on the night the prospect of going all the way out to the New Theatre in Bromley, which would probably have cost him the best part of an hour from central London in heavy traffic, was just too much of a schlep, and he sloped off for a Chinese meal instead.

Or maybe *The Rivals* simply wasn't one of his favourite plays – even a version of it starring yours truly, fully endorsed by the Beatles' own Brian Epstein, and additionally featuring the talents of Lennard Pearce.

Yes, *that* Lennard Pearce. A decade and a half before I warmly shook Lennard by the hand in a little room at the BBC at the first read-through of episode one of *Only Fools and Horses*, the pair of us had been onstage together for a fortnight in a Bromley Rep production.

Lennard played Lucius O'Trigger and the pair of us had a scene together where he threw his arm round the shoulders of my character, Bob Acres, and explained to him the arrangements for a pistol duel, while Bob Acres visibly quailed and shrivelled at the prospect.

We were well down the road on making the series before Lennard and I remembered this encounter, the penny belatedly dropping for us one day: 'Hang on, don't I know you from somewhere . . . ?'

Anyway, maybe the fact that this version of *The Rivals* contained not one but two future members of a leading British sitcom, plus, as it happened, a young and dashing

Martin Jarvis, was not enough in itself to tweak Fernald's interest.

Or maybe Fernald *did* come and see *The Rivals*, took one look at my Bob Acres and decided I wasn't worth bothering with. But that Martin Jarvis, on the other hand . . .

The fact is, I simply don't know. The only thing I can tell you for sure is that all of this back-room chit-chat was complete news to me in 2024. My ears did not burn at the time, the way they are meant to when people talk about you in your absence, and which would have been useful of them. Nothing about the scheme was ever communicated to me and nothing ever arose from it. I carried on in blissful ignorance, with my ears at the usual room temperature, and completed the year of my repertory contract at Bromley.

By which time, I can honestly tell you, the long black limousine of fame – ordered by Brian Epstein or anybody else – had certainly not come calling for me. Indeed, when that repertory contract ran out, in September 1966, a year after Epstein sent his letter, I directly hit a dry patch and had to go back to being an electrician for a bit to make ends meet.

I humbly rang Bob Bevel, my former partner in the business. This is Bob, from whom I had formally separated just twelve months previously, leaving him my half of the business in exchange for my van, and saying (in so many words), 'Sayonara, old chum – I'm on my way to the stars, me.' And now Bob was hearing me on the line saying, 'I don't suppose you've got any spare work on, have you?'

And luckily for me Bob had just taken on a big job on a new building in Elstree and he was able to use me for a few weeks.

But so much for my big career launch. A year after summoning the courage to take the plunge into show business's raging waters, I was back where I started, standing on the bank, dripping wet and looking a bit sheepish.

Or to be more literal, I was up a ladder in a pair of dusty overalls on a building site fifteen miles north of London with a bundle of wire and a screwdriver.

And where was Brian Epstein then, eh?

You will have heard people say: 'It's all about contacts.' And it's clearly true that knowing somebody who can open a door for you or have a word somewhere is sometimes a huge advantage. How could that not occasionally be the case – not just in show business but in all walks of life?

Like the old joke says: nepotism gets a bad name, but some of my best friends in the business have been nepotists.*

However, I'm here to argue that that well-rubbed expression 'it's not what you know, it's who you know' can't be relied upon *all* the time. Certainly I would suggest that what you know will probably always be useful to you, on top of who you know – whereas who you know won't necessarily amount to anything at all.

* At least, I *think* this is an old joke. I might just have made it up. Either way, you're more than welcome.

Why, as my tale above declares: sometimes who you know can be the manager of the Beatles at the very peak of his powers and the mountain still won't move one way or the other.

Incidentally, that Brian Epstein production, *A Smashing Day*, duly opened at the New Arts Theatre in Covent Garden the following January, with a 21-year-old Hywel Bennett in the leading role, and featuring some specially composed musical numbers, performed on guitar and harmonica.

The guitarist? Someone called Ben Kingsley.

The harmonica player? Someone called Robert Powell.

I wonder what became of those two . . .*

* * *

It will always seem remarkable to me that I emerged from Lodge Lane and became a TV actor. It's remarkable, really, that I emerged from Lodge Lane at all.

Certainly you would have to say that 2 February 1940 was not an optimal time to be born into the world if your family happened to live in a terraced house in north London. World

---

* And in case you don't know, Robert Powell, stepping away from his harmonica, later produced a lastingly memorable performance as Jesus Christ, and Ben Kingsley, putting down his guitar, later produced a lastingly memorable and, indeed, Oscar-winning performance as Mahatma Gandhi, so I think we can say that, in every sense, both of them went on to bigger things.

War II was just under way and the German air force seemed to have some fairly radical plans for the area.

What we now think of as the Blitz began on 7 September that year, when I had just turned seven months old and was therefore not in a position to do very much about it. On that particular opening night – 'Black Saturday', as it came to be called – German bombers came for London, dropping 843 bombs, killing 430 people and injuring 1,600. It was merely the first of fifty-seven consecutive nights of attacks on the capital city, with a few daytime sorties thrown in for good measure.

Now, as a babe in arms at that point, I was no doubt aware at some level of these developments as a series of interesting, and most certainly alarming, noises. But otherwise I wouldn't have been concerned with too much that was going on out there in the world beyond the end of my nose. I do frequently wonder about my parents in those years, though, with this baby to look after, and how they felt the first time the air-raid siren sounded.

The protocol was pretty clear regarding best conduct at this moment. The government's announcements over the wireless and in the cinemas had carefully informed people, in the usual crisp and precise tones which public information films went in for, that, upon the sounding of the siren, 'You must get under cover at once. You must not stand staring up at the sky.'

Sound advice, that, you would have to say. And I'm sure

my parents sensibly heeded it – unlike, funnily enough, two Welsh cousins of mine, who legendarily came up to London for a weekend in this period, with the express desire to see what was going on. Moreover, when the eerie sound of an approaching doodlebug was heard, they jumped out into the street, in direct contravention of the official wisdom, to try and catch a glimpse of it.*

A city break in London in the early 1940s? You'd have to say that most of the traffic at that time would have been going in the other direction. But not my cousins. It was as though the war was a hot musical or something. They weren't going to wait for it to tour – they were going to catch it in London.

For my parents, however, any sense that were living in a tourist attraction would have been tempered by a noise that became eerily familiar over those weeks and months: the menacing throb and whine of approaching aircraft bearing their heavy loads. At which point they would withdraw, holding me, to their sheltering point, beneath the kitchen table.

Around 20,000 bombs fell on London alone in the months after Black Saturday. Other cities up and down the UK took their share of the pummelling, too, but for London it peaked

---

* The doodlebug was a flying bomb, a motorised V1. Accordingly, the noise you didn't want to hear directly overhead wasn't the doodlebug's motor; it was the doodlebug's motor stopping.

on the night of 10 May 1941, when German planes dropped 711 tons of high explosives and more than 2,000 incendiary bombs.

Nearly one and a half thousand Londoners were killed in that one raid alone, and how my family weren't among them, I simply don't know. I've traced the bomb damage on the maps and records, and the neighbouring streets all took hits. One bomb struck the back of the nearby Gaumont Cinema, one hit Percy Road, one dropped the other side of Woodside Park underground station, and one fell at the bottom end of Lodge Lane, near to where it joins Gainsborough Road. But our strip of road sat there untouched, like there was some kind of charm over it. And maybe there was.

What a time, though, for my mum to be trying to look after a tiny infant. As if the arrival of a baby doesn't throw a household into disarray enough on its own, without a hostile foreign agent staging a reign of terror from the skies on a nightly basis. But my mother just got on with it, I guess, as people did, having little choice.

I was lastingly struck by a film clip from that era showing a woman in London opening her front door in the morning to take in the milk and casually kicking off the doorstep a few bits of broken slate which had obviously been flung there by the previous night's carnage.

That clash of the shocking and the completely mundane – ordinary life somehow finding a way to go on amid the fear and the destruction – was the story of London lives in those years of war. It was certainly the story of my family, and each of us, in our different ways, took that experience forward with us.

Mind you, we had far worse than a few bits of slate falling onto our house. I've told this story before, but I think it bears telling again. It's quite the tale . . .

One day a neighbour whose house backed onto ours came round and said, 'You won't believe it! There's a chicken on your roof!'

My mum certainly didn't believe it. But she went out the back into the yard and had a look up, and it seemed to be true. A whole, raw, oven-ready chicken was lying on the tiles.

How could you explain that? The local butcher must have taken a hit. Or maybe the butcher's van. Or perhaps just somebody's kitchen, flinging up the contents of the larder. But what a piece of luck! It had rained food! A joint from heaven! There was no turning your nose up at free meat in the middle of a war.

Except, as closer inspection eventually revealed, it wasn't a chicken at all. It was part of a human arm.

Thank heavens for the wardens who came straight round with their ladder, is all I'll say, because I don't suppose my mother or father would have been especially keen to fetch that gruesome item off the roof.

Wince-inducing stories are everywhere when you read about that era. And so are stories of astonishing bravery in the face of those wince-inducing things – tales of people who didn't just wince, in fact, but found from somewhere the strength to perform despite the wincing.

One of my favourites is the tale of the Royal Engineer bomb disposal expert, Lieutenant Robert Davies, who was sent to deal with a massive unexploded bomb that had got itself wedged in a crater, about eight feet below ground level, right underneath St Paul's Cathedral.

Davies quickly realised that the bomb could not be defused: the operation would have been too complex in the circumstances and too dangerous. Nor could this evil item be destroyed where it lay because it would have obliterated the cathedral, along with everything and everyone else in the vicinity. So the only option was to dig the thing out and take it away.

Obviously this was an extremely delicate procedure: you can't just go shovelling out a freshly landed, unexploded bomb and dumping it in a skip for collection by the council next bin day. One false move with the trowel could have set the bomb off, with catastrophic consequences for London's landmark building and, by extension, for the morale of the entire city. And Davies and his team wouldn't have come off too brightly, either.

Oh, and just to make things *really* complicated, there were live electrical cables all over the place in that crater, and a ruptured gas main.

This tense act of excavation took three whole days.

Afterwards, with the offending item now gently lifted into the back of a lorry, but still representing a major threat in a densely populated area, Davies insisted on driving it away himself, in order to spare his colleagues from risking their lives any further.

We can only imagine how nerve-jangling that drive must have been – Davies alone at the wheel, with several tons of the Luftwaffe's finest airborne munitions sitting in the back just behind him.

Remember that the London streets, on account of the merciless peppering they were getting from above, would not have been without their share of potholes in those days.

Actually, they're not without them now, either, as I discovered the other day when I drove in to see the dentist. As ever, he fixed me up very nicely, but by the time I got back home I'd been rattled around so much I practically needed to see him again.

Anyway, those road surfaces would have been even worse in the forties, if you can imagine it, when they had a full-scale war to deal with rather than merely neglect. So Davies very carefully piloted that lorry between the holes, through the city and on a six-mile trip out east to the deserted area of Hackney Marshes, which are now famous as a venue for large numbers of weekend football matches, but which were then a designated 'bomb cemetery' where unexploded items were being taken to receive a hopefully harmless send-off.

Davies took the bomb into the middle of the marshes,

withdrew and remotely detonated it. Whereupon the monster blew a crater thirty metres wide, again making everyone pause to reflect on what might have been. Davies and his team became 'the boys who saved St Paul's' and he was awarded the George Cross for his troubles. Such was the extraordinary selfless heroism taking place in those days, instinctively in many cases, which only makes it seem the more miraculous to me. And it was going on all over the country.

Every cloud has a silver lining, though – even, if you're lucky, the clouds that have bombs falling out of them. None of us would have had anything good to say about it at the time. But afterwards, when all was safe and the national mood was on the upswing . . . well, I have to say, we kids loved what bombing had done with the place.

You see, all those raids had granted us prepubescent herberts an unrivalled wonderland on which to perform those activities that small boys seem to have enjoyed since time immemorial: building dens and throwing bits of brick at each other.*

I know people will want to make a claim for the Harry Potter World theme parks, and I see where those people are coming from. But let me tell you from experience: when it comes to hours of top-class entertainment, with fun and

---

* Reminds me of a joke: what's red and bad for your teeth?
Answer: a house brick.

laughter guaranteed and a touch of magic sprinkled on top, there's an enormous amount to be said for the gap where a couple of terraced houses used to be until the German air force came along.

Sometimes you'd find buried treasure on those sites, too – pennies, jewellery, ornaments, intriguing pieces of metal that could be repurposed as weapons. That's if they hadn't already been picked clean by the kids who got there before you.

Seriously, though, it was all about making the best of your circumstances, I guess. And time and again, we humans, in all our glorious resilience, turn out to be pretty good at that. As a kid, I had a fair bit of energy about me, and the usual child's appetite for danger. Like pretty much all the small boys of my acquaintance back then, I was constitutionally incapable of seeing a shed or garage roof without asking myself, 'I wonder if I could jump off that without breaking anything and/or anyone.' And more often than not, I found I could.

And for the other times, there was the accident and emergency department at the local hospital. I'm thinking in particular here of the occasion my leg and a plank with a rusty nail sticking out of it had an unscheduled coming together. Not pretty to look at, but no lasting harm done, thankfully. Or not to me, anyway. The nail, I believe, never worked again.

But despite all that physical recklessness, I was small and slight and didn't take up much space, and I was a little too shy and hesitant to be one of the major mischief-makers. I left that to some of the others in the gang. I always had half a mind on the consequences so I wasn't very often in trouble.

However, I can say this much: I was almost permanently in rubble. The condition of the local area saw to that. And I was delighted to be so.

So somehow we did survive – and more than that, we thrived. There's a story I always go back to when I'm thinking about my background and the era I came out of, and the ways in which it definitely shaped me. And perhaps this story could be said to contain the message of this book in a nutshell, or at least in a few paragraphs.

It's the one where my dad is cycling to work, as usual, on one of those early-morning rides. And this is in wartime, during the blackout, so the streets are properly dark – the kind of darkness that's almost thick enough to touch.

And, like a good citizen, my dad has fitted a hood to his battery-powered bicycle headlamp so that its beam is angled downwards and it merely provides a small, faint cone of light on the road just ahead of him.

This modified bike-light system is perfect if your purpose is to avoid offering up any kind of illuminated guidance which might assist hostile bombing forces overhead. But it is, of course, next to useless for the road-going cyclist who wishes to see his way ahead.

Yet none of this really represents any kind of problem for my dad, who has done this journey from Southgate to

Billingsgate via Highgate Hill (and home again) a million times, in all weathers, and knows these roads like he knows the back of his hand. He could ride this route blindfold – which he pretty much is, given the conditions.

And then, all of a sudden and without warning, the earth opens up and swallows him. Or, at any rate, my dad plummets, bike and all, into a deep, freshly made bomb crater, completely invisible to him in the darkness.

One minute you're pedalling smoothly down life's highway and the next moment, through no fault of your own, the road disappears from underneath you. There's a lesson and a giant golden nugget of truth right there, no question about it. But it's not the main one I want to take away from this episode.

Because in due course my dad's cries for help from the bottom of this considerable pit are answered by a couple of air-raid wardens – who, of course, when they work out where the shouts are coming from and peer down into the black abyss at this poor stranded fishmonger and his mangled bicycle, assume they are witnessing some kind of miracle.

'Blimey! The bomb must have dropped right on top of him – and he survived!'

A perfectly natural misunderstanding. But anyhow, they haul my dad and his bike up to the surface – and this is the bit of the story that I think merits our special attention as we reflect together in these pages on the virtues of cultivating a positive attitude on our journey down life's bumpy road.

Restored to street level after his presumably quite alarming and also painful spell in solitary confinement at the bottom of a newly crafted bomb crater, my dad has only one thing on his mind. He dusts himself down, he straightens his bike's front wheel, and he cycles on to work.

And it's at that point, surely, dear reader, that my humble dad the fishmonger becomes a role model for us all.

CHAPTER FIVE

*Of silver screens, shortbread biscuits and
the eternal ghost of Derek Trotter*

S*till Open All Hours* wasn't the only project of mine that
got wiped out by the pandemic. Something much bigger
also went down the pan. A feature film I was all lined up for.

Oh yes indeed: the movies. Hollywood!

Well, actually I'm not sure. Maybe Borehamwood.

But we were deep into discussions, that much I can tell you.
By which I mean there had been a meeting.

Big movie, apparently. Kind of a ghost story, if I understood
the pitch properly. Glittering all-star cast, definitely – subject
to confirmation, of course, as these things inevitably are.

Bound for Netflix, don't you know. Or possibly Netflix –
maybe somewhere else. Destined, surely, to be the most enormous smash at the box office and make vast inroads into the
streaming market, ensuring that it would be Milky Bars all
round for everyone involved.

Potentially.

What can I say? I was intrigued.

'Fantastic,' I'd said, in between sips of cappuccino at that meeting. 'If you can get it off the ground, I'm in.'

But of course the next thing I knew, Boris Johnson was broadcasting to the nation in front of a podium marked 'Hands, Face, Space' – or was it 'Hands, Knees, Boops-a-daisy'? Something like that. And everything was cancelled.

And once again my prospects for that big breakthrough on the silver screen were on ice, along with the plans for my Malibu beach house. (Nothing too flash; 15,000 square feet or so, ocean views, motorised glass windows – you know the kind of thing.)

Mind you, when it comes to the dangling of film roles under my nose, I have discovered that it pays to retain a high degree of scepticism if you possibly can, and try not to count your chickens and/or your Malibu beach houses. In the film industry, one very quickly understands, an awful lot of talk has to take place before anyone starts actually filming anything. And in my experience, quite frequently it's only the talk that takes place and nobody ends up filming anything at all.

Or not with me in it.

Let me demonstrate. Here are two stories from the recent past relating to your humble author and the tantalising offer of parts in potentially blockbusting movies.

Story one: a handful of years ago a producer got in touch to request a meeting with me, and we duly got together in the lounge of a nice hotel, as seems to be the general pattern, where cappuccinos were soon arriving and a plate of shortbread biscuits was turning up, which is never to be sniffed at.

We supped our coffees and shot the breeze a while, and then the producer set down his cup and leaned forward slightly, which is always the moment when you know the pitch is coming.

The producer asked me if I had read a novel called *The Unlikely Pilgrimage of Harold Fry* by a writer named Rachel Joyce, and, with a mouthful of shortbread, I confessed that I had not.

So the producer told me about it.

It was the story of an elderly man, living in retirement in Devon, who gets a letter from an old acquaintance, who tells him she is dying in a hospice, miles away in Scotland, and doesn't have long to live. She's writing to say goodbye.

And he writes back to her, but he's unhappy with the letter that he's written – that he can't make the words work, that it doesn't say enough. Nevertheless, he goes out to post the letter because it's all he's got.

And then the idea grips him that maybe the letter *isn't* all he's got, and he walks past the postbox, and keeps walking, all the way to Scotland and the hospice and the dying woman's bedside.

Meanwhile his wife is back at home, worrying about where he's gone and . . . well, I won't spoil the rest of it.

But I thought it sounded great.

'I want to make the film of this book,' the producer said, 'and I want you to be in it as Harold Fry – as the elderly man on the pilgrimage.'

I had no hesitation at all.

'Fantastic,' I said. 'If you can get it off the ground, I'm in.'

Please now imagine some years going by. Whole years. Moons wax and wane. A global pandemic comes and goes. The prime minister changes, many times. *Love Island* happens again and again and again. In that period, I hear nothing at all from anybody on the subject of Harold Fry, pilgrimages or walking to Scotland without telling your wife. All is silence.

And then, in 2023, I'm casually browsing a newspaper in a dentist's waiting room and my eye falls on an advert for one of that week's new cinema releases: *The Unlikely Pilgrimage of Harold Fry* starring Jim Broadbent.

'An incredibly beautiful film,' says one of the reviews quoted on the ad. 'Immediately one of the great movies about ageing and regret,' says another.

Lowering the paper slowly to my lap and equally slowly raising my head, I stare across the room and enter a state of what I can only describe as mournful reverie, broken eventually by a woman's voice.

'The dentist will see you now, sir.'

Look, I completely understand. Jim Broadbent is a superb

actor with a major background in film.* Who wouldn't want him in their movie in a role like that?

It's just that . . . well, what about that meeting? Didn't we have an arrangement here? Where was *I* when they were making 'one of the great movies about ageing and regret'? I thought that was meant to be *me* doing the ageing and the regretting.

When I look a little closer, though, I also realise that I don't recognise the name of the producer on this new movie. It's not the person who saw me. Anyway, I retreat and quietly nurse my bruises – from this development and also, of course, from the dentistry. (Installation of a crown: never fun.)

Here's the second story in this vein.

A producer requests a meeting – a different producer this time. Again, this is some years ago. Again, we gather in the lounge of a nice hotel, and again, cappuccinos arrive and that most welcome plate of shortbread. And again, after the obligatory period of supping and breeze-shooting, this producer sets his cup down, leans forward and pitches me an idea for a film.

It's based on a true story about an elderly gentleman in an old people's home. He's an ex-serviceman, this gentleman,

---

* He's also, as you may know, one of the five or so people who turned down the role of Derek Trotter, for which decision I have cause to be eternally grateful to him. Later, of course, Jim was brilliant in the series as Del's nemesis, the chillingly scary DI Slater.

who fought at Dunkirk as part of the British Expeditionary Force in 1939 and 1940. A big anniversary is coming up on the site of the battle in France, and naturally he's desperate to be a part of it.

But they tell him he's not well enough and he can't go.

He's not having that, though. He escapes from the care home when the nursing staff aren't looking and sets off for France, on foot, on his own, determined to be reunited one last time with some of the people he served with.

'What would you think about playing the lead in that movie?' the producer asks.

And what I think, of course, is that I would absolutely love it. What a part! And what a great story.

'Fashashic!' I say – which was meant to be 'Fantastic!' but it's not an easy word to say with a mouthful of shortbread. I finish chewing and swallow. 'If you can get it off the ground, I'm in.'

We shake hands firmly and go our separate ways.

Once again, years pass. Once again I mean a number of years. The world spins on its axis, tyrants come and go, gases explode in the galaxy and form entirely new planets, and all is silence on the subject of me playing an elderly war veteran giving his carers the slip and stepping out for France.

And eventually once again it's 2023 and I'm opening a newspaper and, clearly, yes, they *could* get that movie off the ground, but not with the producer I met and not with me on board, because now here's this new release, heading to a cinema near me: *The Great Escaper*, starring Glenda Jackson and . . . Michael Caine.

Michael Caine!

Again, don't get me wrong, I am by no means disputing this casting decision. Michael Caine has appeared in more than 160 films and won two Oscars – and as Daphne the under-housemaid will no doubt quite gladly tell you, even my extensive shelf of industry baubles and accolades doesn't extend to any of those.

And while we're mentioning it, Glenda Jackson was no slouch, either.

By contrast, my major motion picture background extends to . . . well, we'll come on to that in a minute. For now, let's just say that I can hardly feel aggrieved that, unbeknown to myself, I have gone head-to-head with Michael Caine in the fight for a leading role in a film and lost.

But . . . well, you know what I'm going to say here: we had a meeting! I thought that was going to be *me* escaping from the care home and going to look for my Dunkirk chums.

It's the hope that kills you.

The writer Neil Gaiman once said that he never believes his books are actually going to be made into films until he's sitting in the cinema with a box of popcorn in his lap and the lights have gone down and the titles have come up. *Then* he'll believe it.

That seems a very wise approach to me, and one I shall be attempting to adapt to my own situation forthwith.

My problem in this area, clearly, is that I find myself in that typical bind faced by job applicants since time immemorial. 'Wanted: experienced person,' say the advertisements. But how are you going to get that experience if they're only hiring experienced people? That's been my position in relation to movies. If only I had some films under my belt, then I might be able to get some films under my belt.

That said, I do have *some* film credits on my CV. It's just that the credits in question . . .

Well, what am I trying to say here?

Let me put it this way: I would love to be able to declare that my collected film work on DVD would make for an elegant shelf of high-class cinematic experiences to browse among of an evening. I fear, however, that it may look more like the contents of a box pulled out from under a table at a car boot sale.

I mean, I'm not saying you can't turn up some absolute gems at a car boot sale.

But judge for yourselves.

Things started out quite promisingly in this area, actually. Late in 1970, with very little on my CV at the time, I auditioned for a part in a film adaptation of Dylan Thomas's *Under Milk Wood*, and came away with a role: Nogood Boyo. That was enormously pleasing for me. For one thing, I love that piece of writing and always have. For another, it was a chance for me to appear in something paying explicit honour to Wales, the land of my father – or rather, to be strictly accurate, the land of my mother, Olwen Jones, who was originally from Merthyr Tydfil.

Filming took place the following year in Fishguard – and not in Laugharne where Dylan Thomas was living when he wrote the piece, a decision which apparently caused some noses to be wrinkled among the Dylan Thomas purists. It was said at the time that this was the equivalent of filming James Joyce's *Dubliners* in Birmingham.

I'm not sure that's fair, though, is it? Thomas might have been living in Laugharne when he wrote *Under Milk Wood*, but he didn't set it there. He set it in the made-up Welsh town of Llareggub.*

And anyway, movies are always transplanting things and pretending somewhere is somewhere else. Wait until those purists find out how many westerns were shot in Spain.

Or, for that matter, that the lion's share of the Peckham scenes in *Only Fools* were shot in Bristol.

Anyway, from the cast's point of view, the problem wasn't the location (which was perfectly lovely, in fact) so much as the time of year – a freezing, wet February which didn't exactly make for a comfortable experience for those of us involved in the film's many outdoor scenes. And it especially didn't make for comfort during the outdoor scenes that involved clothing removal.

* If you want to decode the mystery of the town name of Llareggub, write it backwards.

189

In one scene, a dream sequence, Ruth Madoc and I had to frolic in the sea: cold enough for me, fully clothed, in trousers and a woolly jumper, but viciously cold for Ruth, in a corset and, moreover, pregnant at the time. On another day, which was at least clear and bright, Susan Penhaligon ended up shooting a sequence out on the hillside, unbuttoned and casually doodling on herself with lipstick. It was so cold the lipstick kept snapping and needing to be replaced. True story.

Susan, incidentally, had this to say to an interviewer from the Dylan Thomas Society newsletter who asked her not long ago for her recollections of that film shoot:

'I also remember the young David Jason, before he was known, fooling around in the bar, being very funny. I thought, he's going to be successful one day. True.'

Ah, Susan, bless you for that. If only my latent talents had managed to burn themselves more clearly into the celluloid on that occasion. And if only I'd had the chance to be very funny on film rather than in the bar. Save your best work, is surely the lesson here.

Susan, let's just add, auditioned for her part in *Under Milk Wood* on the set in Wales, when filming had already began. She assumed she would be seen indoors somewhere, so pitched up in seventies casualwear – hot pants and a pair of knee-high pink boots – only to discover that her audition was in the middle of a muddy field and that wellies and a boilersuit would probably have been the better wardrobe choice.

Oh well. It's funny to think back to that shoot now: me, Ruth, Susan, all setting out on our various journeys through the acting trade, none of us really in control of what lay ahead, all gamely putting ourselves through it in the hope that bigger things might come our way.

I should say that there were also parts in that *Under Milk Wood* film for Richard Burton and Elizabeth Taylor – film royalty, of course, and also very much NOT bungling beginners at that stage of their careers. So that, at least, got the film noticed.

And Peter O'Toole was blind Captain Cat, wearing a pair of strikingly bright blue prosthetic eyes. But not even the glow cast by these star names could quite redeem the finished item or convert it into the major contribution to the cinematic art form that I had dreamed of it being when I set out for Fishguard with a quickly packed holdall and a burning ambition. The film was patchy and hard to follow, and the general verdict seemed to be that *Under Milk Wood* was written for radio, and that it showed.

No matter. Very swiftly after this, fate again smiled in a beguiling manner and another golden opportunity presented itself. I landed a part in a movie – a British farce – that was going to be shot at Twickenham Film Studios. Better than that, my farcical skills had so impressed at the audition that I was given the leading role.

Yes, I wasn't just going to be *in* this movie, I was going to *star* in this movie.

191

What could possibly go wrong?

This was a film which came out in 1973 called *White Cargo* – although at the point I signed up for it, it was going under the less racy title *Albert's Follies*. I was cast to play Albert Toddey, a meek, Walter Mitty-like office worker who has daydreams about being a James Bond-style agent.

You may detect a parallel here with the set-up for the ITV sitcom that I would later be offered, *The Top Secret Life of Edgar Briggs* – which, you will know if you were paying attention a couple of chapters ago, featured me as a member of Her Majesty's Secret Service who also nurtures wild delusions about his abilities.

I don't know what I must have been projecting in those days. It was as if casting directors took one look at me and thought: 'James Bond – but only in his dreams.'

Quite hurtful, really, those casting directors.

Anyway, *Albert's Follies* looked quite exciting to me on paper. The very funny Hugh Lloyd was in the cast, with whom I had already worked in that Terry Scott sitcom *Hugh and I*. And so was Imogen Hassall, who by this time had earned herself no little fame by appearing in the Hammer House of Horror movie *When Dinosaurs Ruled the Earth* and also alongside all the usual suspects in *Carry on Loving*, appearances which had seen her earn from the tabloid papers the nickname 'the Countess of Cleavage'.

This was all, shall we say, very much of its time, and one's ability to chortle about it now must be sobered by many things, not least the fact that, only a few years after this, in 1980, poor Imogen took her own life, at the age of just thirty-eight.

Also in that cast: David Prowse, who in this movie played someone called Harry, but who would later have a little more success by playing someone called Darth Vader in the *Star Wars* films.

Well, at least someone in this movie travelled on to Hollywood and the high life.

Filming coincided unhelpfully with my run in *No Sex Please – We're British* and I still shake my head to reflect how I managed to combine these two commitments without permanently straining something. In terms of exertion, that *No Sex Please* role was more physically demanding than any I had taken on – or that I would *ever* take on, actually. Six nights a week, with matinees on Thursday and Saturday, I was onstage, leaping and diving around and hanging off bits of the scenery like an idiot.

Then I was getting up at dawn and flashing out west to Twickenham Film Studios for a day of even more leaping and diving around like an idiot, before flopping into the back of a taxi and speeding back into the West End in time to get changed, made up and ready for curtain-up at 7.30. This went on for two months.

I'm not entirely sure what I was running on, but ambition was clearly a part of the mix, and ambition is the most extraordinary fuel, clearly. Then again, why *wouldn't* I have felt energised? Passing through the barrier at Twickenham every morning, getting the nod from the commissaire, heading to make-up and wardrobe, walking onto the set . . . I felt I was on the escalator leading directly to international stardom. I had well and truly arrived.

And what a great thing all of this was to be able to float casually in front of your friends and colleagues.

'Tea on Wednesday? No, I can't, I'm afraid. Got to be on set that afternoon, unfortunately. Yeah, I'm shooting a movie . . . Say again? . . . Oh, no, nothing much . . . just the leading role . . .'

Unfortunately, the movie in question was a complete and utter catastrophe. It was under-funded, under-rehearsed, under-cooked and many other words, I don't doubt, with 'under' at the start of them.

Did I realise as much at the time? I don't think I did. Being so inexperienced in this realm, I had no real idea what this film was going to look like when it was put together. I was just doing my scenes, as instructed, getting the job done, and leaving it to others to work their magic in the edit suite. There was no time, really, to reflect or sit back and take a view of the situation, because I was either working, in the back of a taxi, or asleep. Except for the occasions when I was asleep in the back of a taxi, which were many.

Plus I was so smitten with the idea that I, a humble stage actor, so early in his career, had landed up in a leading role in a movie that I kind of wafted through it all in a state of blithe wonder.

But the resulting film really was the most gigantic lemon. It was scene after scene of slapstick comedy that didn't land, wrapped around a convoluted plot that made little sense – which is not, I'm sure you will sense, a recipe for box-office gold.

Later, in what seems to have been a panicked attempt to provide at least *something* that people might enjoy watching and which might get the film talked about, the director threw in a random, soft-core sex scene – not involving me, I'm rather relieved to add.

And the reception? Well, permit me to quote from a review:

> A wretchedly unfunny attempt at a comedy in the Norman Wisdom style, faithfully resurrecting every 'rude' gag, from falling trousers to laboriously climbing (at great risk to manhood) over a gate that proves to be unlocked. Particularly embarrassing is an effort to beef up the sexploitation angle with what is possibly the coyest sex scene ever shot; mercifully, there is every sign that the film has been heavily cut.

That was from *The Monthly Film Bulletin*. You can see why they call it a 'bulletin'. And that critic hadn't been persuaded to put his gun down by the inserted-sex-scene ruse, clearly.

Here was a deeply deflating lesson for me personally in the wake of all the excitement and the anticipation that had coursed through me during the making of that movie: you can get up at dawn to risk your manhood going over an unlocked gate in the name of entertainment and a place in history, and it will earn you nothing but a slagging-off in *The Monthly Film Bulletin.*

But there was another, more lasting lesson, too: namely, that the quality of the piece is the thing to get excited about, and not the ideas you might have about where that piece might take you. Only the work you're doing matters, really, and all the rest is distraction – and beyond your power to control anyway.

Or to use my chosen phrase again: it's the journey, not the arrival.

So that was my big-screen starring debut. I crept away and nursed my crushed dreams.

Things went a little quiet on the film front after that little debacle. But I did get another stab at it a few years later. In 1978, Graham Chapman from *Monty Python* invited me to star with him in *The Odd Job*, a film he was co-producing and for which he had written the screenplay, expanding on an original piece by Bernard McKenna.

It's a comedy about a man who falls into a deep depression when his wife leaves him and who, being a bit squeamish about suicide, hires somebody to bump him off. But then life takes a turn for the better, his wife suddenly comes back to him, and he cheers up and changes his mind.

Unfortunately, though, the contract is still out and can't

be cancelled, so he's now trying to avoid getting assassinated by his own appointed assassin – who's a bit of a bungler, as it happens, and keeps offing the wrong people by mistake.

It's a fun set-up, and I had been in the original, thirty-minute television version of this piece, in 1970, playing the assassin, the odd-job man of the title, opposite Ronnie Barker, and I guess that experience is what swung the job for me the best part of a decade later. I've learned since that Graham was hoping that Keith Moon, the drummer from The Who, would play opposite him as the assassin. But Moon proved unavailable, so Graham chose me.

This is, I strongly believe, the only occasion in my career in which my name has been considered interchangeable with that of a fully paid-up, card-carrying wild man of rock. I'm rather proud of that, and in celebration I offer you the following knotty teaser for your next pub quiz:

What connects the actor David Jason with Keith Moon, the late drummer of The Who? Is it:
a) They were both guilty of dropping television sets into swimming pools.
b) They both enjoyed placing sticks of dynamite in hotel room lavatories and igniting them.
c) They were both offered the part of Clive in *The Odd Job*.

Anyway, *The Odd Job* came out and was met, so far as I recall, largely with indifference. The feeling was that in the process of expanding on the original TV play into a full-length feature, it had become a bit thin.

Another damp film experience for your author.

And beyond that one? Well, I'm sorry to say the CV rather tails off at this point. Soon after *The Odd Job* came out, the television work picked up and barrelled on and I had that to occupy myself with and be very glad about, and even the idea of exploring potential film business had to take a back seat.

Unless TV movies count. If so, we can throw in *March in the Windy City*, which I mentioned in the previous chapter. But as I myself can only remember the bit with the gun in the hotel corridor, it might be stretching it a bit.

The thing is, the film dream lingered. It was apparently indestructible in that sense. Even through those times when I was otherwise occupied, that little aspiration was always in there somewhere, waiting to come out in a quiet moment or play across the back of my eyelids at night. Among the members of my tribe, I would hardly be unusual in this. Indeed, I don't suppose there's any actor who ever quite stops wondering whether just round the corner lies the film role that's going to change *everything*. And until then, it's a thwarted longing – the greener grass on the other side of the fence, the land unconquered.

And guess what: in my case, here comes that dream again.

It happened at the very low point of my post-pandemic barren phase, the point where, with the diary empty and showing no sign of filling again, I'd practically given up hope.

Picture the scene. It was a dull Tuesday afternoon. By now I had done everything to occupy myself. I was up to my chin in finished wooden models with a mechanical element. I had made as many riding-boot lamps as any man could reasonably be expected to and I had bottled enough tomato chutney to fuel Hannibal and his army across the Alps, including the elephants.

Furthermore, I had mastered not only sourdough-bread baking and chess, but also the piano and the sousaphone, after which, bored again, I had learned to play the piano and the sousaphone *at the same time.**

In short, I had exhausted the options. I had resorted to standing miserably at the window and peering off into the distance in the hope of spotting, on the very furthest horizon, a small cloud of dust that might finally signal salvation in the form of some approaching work.

And what do you know? There, on that far horizon, was that cloud of dust, and it was getting closer and closer, and larger and larger, until it was near enough that I could make out the figure at the centre of it.

It couldn't be, could it? Yes, it was! A film producer! Another one! With a request for a meeting!

And proposing, obviously, that we have that meeting in

---

* This is a joke. I cannot play the piano, or the sousaphone. I couldn't play either of them before the pandemic, and I couldn't play either of them afterwards. Ditto chess and sourdough baking. It's as well to be clear about these things.

the lounge of a nice hotel. With cappuccinos, naturally. And shortbread, of course.

Reader, it wasn't over after all. It never is! Against all the odds, at the point of no return, a solitary flower had bloomed in the desert.

And actually there were some immediately encouraging signs about this particular approach. Omens, you could almost say. For one thing, upon request, they sent me a hard copy of the script – on actual paper. That's quite rare these days. Mostly you'll get sent a file attached to an email. And I absolutely understand that that's a far better thing from the point of view of our forestry. But I'm old-fashioned in this regard, I'm afraid. I need to have pages to turn over.

For another thing, they sent me the *complete* script. You'd be surprised how many people just send you the pages with the lines for your proposed character on them, as if that's all you're going to want to see. That's no good for me. I want to know the whole story. I want to find out how my character fits in and what else is going on. It's been the same with everything I've done for television, too, incidentally. It surprises me that other actors clearly don't feel the need for this.

Never mind, though. These were good signs, is all I'm saying. I repaired to the nice hotel, I supped the coffee, and I listened to the pitch.

It's about an elderly man, a former motorcycle champion whose feats are largely forgotten and who one day . . .

But I'd better not say any more for fear of jinxing it. And

I was born on 2 February 1940, not an optimal moment if your family happened to live in a terraced house in north London. World War II was just under way and the German air force seemed to have some fairly radical plans for my area. I was lucky enough to fly in a Spitfire for the documentary *David Jason: Battle of Britain* in 2010 and pay tribute to all those who lost their lives in that terrible conflict. Flying over the White Cliffs of Dover in that iconic aircraft brought a tear to my eye.

Who said you can't find the secret to life at the bottom of the deep blue sea? Diving has been a great passion of mine, giving me a sense of wonderment and freedom. Here I am filming a documentary, *David Jason In His Element*, at the Christ of the Abyss statue in Key Largo. If Christ was supposed to catch me in his open arms, he missed!

On location with Nick Lyndhurst in Florida for 'Miami Twice', the 1991 Christmas special of *Only Fools and Horses*. We were living our best lives and felt like real cool dudes. Happy days!

Credit: Trinity Mirror / Mirrorpix / Alamy Stock Photo

Some holiday snaps from a recent trip to Florida (without the cast of *Only Fools and Horses*) – one of my favourite places in the world. Clockwise from top left: my wife Gill, my daughter Sophie, Marilyn Monroe (seen here giving me directions), and Sophie's boyfriend Harvey, who I refer to as the BFG (Big Friendly Giant). Looking at this picture, you can see why!

If they want to do a remake of *Miami Vice*, I have a casting idea …

Bella the rescue dog and Tuffy the Labrador. Who pinched the sausage? 'It wasn't us …'

I've always had a mechanical brain and enjoy making and fixing things. Lockdown allowed me to indulge in these hobbies, or over-indulge, as my wife Gill would put it, as the house filled up with contraptions.

Blending my passion for making things with making fun TV, *David and Jay's Touring Toolshed* was a delight. Meeting passionate and eccentric crafters and tinkerers up and down the UK was the best way to spend a summer. Getting to know Jay better wasn't half bad either.

Back to the start. *Still Open All Hours*, which ran from 2013 to 2019, was a joy and allowed me to revisit my comedy roots. From time to time I was choked up thinking about the wonderful Ronnie Barker and his genius Arkwright.

Credit: WENN Rights Ltd / Alamy Stock Photo

'To begin at the beginning.' That was how the letter began – the most astonishing letter I've ever received, and one that led to a newly discovered daughter, Abi Hill – the daughter I didn't know I had – and her son, Charlie, my first grandson.

of course, as I know all too painfully, this could still turn out to be a mirage.

However, you never know, do you?

'Fantastic!' I again heard myself say at that meeting, having been wise enough to empty my mouth of shortbread first this time. 'If you can get if off the ground, I'm in.'

This is all very exciting, I thought to myself as I drove home. Why, this time next year . . .

Well, actually, if my previous experiences are anything to go by, with *The Pilgrimage of Harold Fry* and *The Great Escaper*, this time next year I'll be watching this film on the telly and Tom Hanks will be starring in it.

But no. Why even entertain that thought at this stage? Let's stay positive. It's a film role, after all. And in relation to those, I'm in a strong position to tell you: hope springs eternal.

*   *   *

The fact that my career, though amply strung with honours in so many humbling ways, has yet to ignite in a blaze of Hollywood glory has yielded one clear benefit over the years. It means I have been able to go to America and be completely unrecognised. And this, you've got to admit, would not so readily have been the case had it – just for example – been me, rather than Tom Cruise, who secured the leading role in the *Mission: Impossible* franchise.

201

Look, you seek your consolations where you can find them, and that's mine.

And actually, this is a very valuable compensation because I love America, and have done ever since I first went there, back in the seventies, visiting a friend who had gone to work in California.

But I think part of why I have grown especially to love it in the meantime is the freedom I get there to blend in with everyone else and totally relax and not have to feel slightly self-conscious, which I often do when I'm out and about in the UK.

Florida was where we went for holidays after Gill and I got together, and when Sophie came along, returning always to the same place by the water which my great friend David Reynolds had steered us towards and which we loved.

Fishing, picnics on boats, teaching Sophie to swim . . . we have lots of fantastic memories there. And in 2024, for the first time in several years (with other things having intervened, such as the pandemic, Sophie's time at university and a sense that it might be sensible to cut down on flying), we went back.

This time it was me, Gill and Sophie plus her boyfriend, who happens to be very tall and towers over me. When we walk together we look like a scene from *The BFG*. It's a little humiliating, if I'm being honest. It rather undermines the powerful authority and mild sense of brooding menace that I would like to be exuding as a father in this situation. But what can you do? So the BFG is what I refer to him as.

Not having flown for a while, I'd forgotten how much of the experience of flying seems designed to put you off flying forever. And I guess that's exactly what the airlines rely on – everybody's forgetfulness.

There's all the business with the security checks, for starters – taking off your shoes and your belt and shuffling into scanners and being told to raise your arms in the air, for all the world as if you're being processed for admittance to prison. None of this stuff was any more fun than I'd remembered it. Not least after my newly acquired hip set off the alarm.

Then, of course, there's the practically cast-iron guarantee that you will be seated on the plane directly behind a child who regards their own seat as a trampoline and has checked in for a good six-hour transatlantic bouncing session. I had one this time whose energy could have powered the plane most of the way to America. At one point I wondered whether my best way forward might be simply to give in – to join her and start bouncing on *my* seat.

Now, of course, it's all very well for children, but if you jump up and down on your plane seat as an adult, they start talking about making an emergency landing and involving the police. So I sat there and did nothing.

Once off the plane, you're still not quite through the stress because you've still got to clear immigration at Miami.

There's frequently a major crowd scene in the immigration hall, with the queue snaking back practically to London again, although this time, at least, we got lucky and walked through pretty quickly. But those US immigration guys can be intimidating at the best of times, so I'm always a bit reflexively anxious as I head to the booth clutching my passport.

The rest of the family had already gone through, so now it was just me standing at the window, smiling in a way that I hoped conveyed beyond all doubt that I was a person of sound character and eminently suitable to be welcomed to the country for a couple of weeks in the sunshine.

The officer looked at me coolly, then he looked at my passport, and then he looked at me again. I could feel my smile beginning to take its toll on my face muscles.

'Hmm,' he said eventually, seeming very sceptical about something. '*Sir* David. Tell me – what is the "Sir" for?'

'Well,' I said, 'it's for acting. I'm an actor. I've been knighted. For acting.'

He carried on looking at me suspiciously.

'What does that mean?'

'Well, it's a ceremony where you kneel and the Queen, as it was at the time, takes a sword and places it on each of your shoulders, and then you stand up.'

He was still looking at me.

'So when was this?'

I said, 'Oh, it was a couple of decades ago now, or thereabouts.'

He thought about this and nodded slowly. Then he reached across his desk, picked up a small notebook and a pen, and pushed them under the glass to me.

'Would you sign this for me?'

The notebook had a slightly tatty cover and very thin pages and a blotter inside it – like an old receipt book. At first I thought this must be another part of the process – a customs declaration or something, another chance for me to state formally that I would not be importing any livestock or trees in my suitcase on this particular occasion.

But no. I opened the notebook and realised that it housed a quite significant collection of autographs.

Well, as a member of the US Border Forces in Miami, you're pretty well placed for autograph hunting, I guess. Who knows what rich celebrity pickings must come past your window in the course of your work, so why wouldn't you?

Also, in the circumstances, who's likely to say no?

Under some of the signatures, my official friend had helpfully written an identifying caption. I flicked through a couple of the pages – and there was Barry Gibb of the Bee Gees.

Extraordinary! Barry, of course, made an appearance in the *Only Fools* Christmas special 'Miami Twice', when he gamely stood on the lawn of his waterside home so that Del could bellow at him from a passing ferry. A lovely man, Barry, a huge *Only Fools* fan – and clearly a former client at some point of my autograph-hunting immigration officer.

'What a coincidence!' I said. 'I worked with Barry Gibb.'

'You worked with Barry Gibb?'

'Yes – right here, in Miami!'

I found a clean page, signed my name and handed the book back to him. His expression had thawed a little. I was a 'Sir' and I had worked with Barry Gibb: I was a respectable addition to his collection.

'Welcome to the United States of America, sir,' he said, handing back my passport. 'And I hope you have a happy time here in Florida.'

I rejoined the family, waiting for me round the corner.

'Why were you so long? We thought you'd been deported.'

'I was starting to worry about that, too,' I said. 'But in fact he just wanted my autograph.'

A set of expressions now met me, even more sceptical than the one my new friend in the booth had worn – as if to say, 'Your autograph? In America? Yeah, right.'

Still, we were in the United States now, and at least from hereon in I could guarantee everyone that there would be no more interruptions. That's why they call it the Land of the Free, after all. I could now shed the metaphorical flat cap of Derek Trotter, bless him, and hang it on the metaphorical peg for a fortnight and we could all have a rest from him.

Because, of course, it's not just unsettling for me, when Del starts attracting attention in places; it's unsettling for the people I'm with, and puts them on edge a bit, too.

So the holiday was happily under way. We settled into our rented house and started reacquainting ourselves with the familiar charm of the place. One of the things I was keenest to do was head back to what had always been my favourite restaurant – a kind of shack by the water with its own little jetty from which you could watch holidaymakers making a royal mess of docking their boats. (Another advantage of anonymity here.)

I was worried that this restaurant might have been swept away by one of the recent hurricanes. But no, it was still there and exactly as it was. My old refuge.

We walked in and began to look for a table. At which point, a voice came from behind me.

'Look who it isn't! It's Del Boy!'

It seemed the place was under new management. Someone from Enfield, apparently.

And the ghost of Derek Trotter had come sailing up the river to haunt me again.

In fact, we had a very nice exchange, me and the new manager. And the food was as good as ever, though there was no mention of ignoring the bill . . . Maybe next time.

And that really *was* the only time that Del got a look-in on this particular holiday. It is extraordinary, though, how far-reaching the effects can be of appearing in a successful British comedy series. Roger Lloyd Pack, who played Trigger, reckoned he could plummet to the bottom of the Mariana

Trench inside a one-man submarine and he would still hear someone down there say 'All right, Dave?'*

All of us on *Only Fools* had to negotiate our own ways around this – the constant recognition, I mean, not the Mariana Trench. Lennard had no problem with people spotting him, and seemed to love every aspect of it. Buster, too, greeted the whole thing like a glorious treat, and probably for similar reasons. The visibility reached both of those two, quite out of the blue, late in their careers, and they enjoyed the warmth of it. John Challis, meanwhile, was a gentleman, with the patience of a saint and answered the endless requests to 'do the Boycie laugh' with wonderful good grace.

And me? Well, I'll admit I found it quite troublesome at times, and I would say that Nick did, too. After a while I developed the feeling that I couldn't go anywhere without Derek Trotter coming along too, and although that was fine up to a point, it also seemed to sound a few alarm bells about the future.

I had to be careful how I talked about this because people could get the wrong impression. It seemed an ungrateful and even bizarre thing to be grumbling at all about a role that had opened so many doors for me.

But it was the doors which that role might now *shut*

* Mariana Trench: no, not a presenter on ITV's *Loose Women*, but the deepest oceanic trench on earth, getting on for seven miles deep at its lowest point and positioned in the Pacific Ocean way out beyond the Philippines, if you're thinking of going.

which started to worry me. If people associated me so firmly with one character, and if that character was instantly what my face meant to people, how was I ever going to get another role?

It's an age-old sitcom-related dilemma, this. How was I ever going to be cast in a serious part as a detective, say (something I had started hankering after playing), if the only person that walked in when I did was Del?

What chance did I have, similarly, of playing a Cambridge head porter in a comic satire, or a captain from the Norfolk Regiment at Gallipoli in a serious BBC drama for screening on Remembrance Day if people most notably associated me with trying to offload a bulk order of dodgy personal massagers? I did seriously have to think quite hard from time to time about how I was going to save my skin, professionally speaking, from the wonderful yet once-seen-never-forgotten nature of Derek Trotter.

I almost felt as though I should be explaining to people in advance that me and Del weren't the same person – that I don't actually talk like him, and I don't actually walk like him. And that I've certainly never tried to pass off a job lot of electric paint-strippers as 'radically designed hairdryers' like him.

Otherwise, you felt you were letting people down by turning up not dressed like Del, and not continually spouting Del-like lines.

And just to be absolutely clear, I *don't* dress like Del,

despite having snaffled one of his sheepskin coats from the wardrobe department at the end of a series as a souvenir. (Very snug, actually. But not terribly stylish, and my wife gently suggested that it was making me look, and slightly smell, like a camel, so that was the end of that.)

Now, that's not to say that there aren't aspects of Del's character that I can relate to, and have even lived a little bit in my own life. For example, just the other day I was remembering a little scam that used to get pulled every now and again when I was an electrician and doing work for the Eastern Electricity Board, a scam I think Del would have appreciated.

Back then there would be jobs on your list for the day that would be rated as non-chargeable, meaning the customer wouldn't be paying for them but the electricity board would be covering the cost of the work themselves. These jobs would be written out on yellow dockets – 'yellow perils', we used to call them.

Now, if it should happen that the customer on a yellow-peril job wasn't home when you called – well, then happy days, because you could still charge the board for the call-out, but, of course, you wouldn't need to do the actual work.

Bingo – a free half-hour had just opened up on your schedule, and you were being paid for it.

And if the customer should be at home, but not hear you when you knocked at the door – well, the same rule applied, obviously, because you would still be able to mark them down in your book as absent, and you would still get your call-out fee, courtesy of the board, and your leisure time.

So, given that this was the case, and that a small loophole was temptingly dangling, were there attempts by visiting electricians on those yellow-peril jobs to knock, shall we say, a little lightly at some of the houses in question?

To *pretend* to knock, even?

And, having 'knocked', did those visiting electricians then slip away to their vans to mark the customer down as out at the time of calling?

And did said electricians take the trouble to make their 'knocking' look as convincing as possible, just in case neighbours were watching, or, indeed, the customers themselves from an unseen vantage point?

Reader, form your own inferences, but such activities may well have been known to occur at the time. Indeed, it's probably the case that some highly convincing amateur-dramatic performances took place at the doors of those yellow-peril customers; the electrician advancing committedly up the path with his toolbox; 'knocking'; stepping back to wait; perhaps even 'knocking' again, before heading back down the path to the van with a shrug and a mildly frustrated expression. And all in the cause of maximum plausibility should they have been spotted trying to get away with one.

Would that the BAFTA committee had been in attendance then.

Now, obviously, with the benefit of mature wisdom, I am by no means condoning this conduct. On the contrary, you are to picture me at this juncture with the most sober and regretful of expressions on my face.

But let me also assert that the view of the electricians back then would have been that they were slyly getting one over on the system, an outcome that would have brought them a little bit of satisfaction to cheer the working day. And the burden, let me insist, would have been borne, not by the individual customer, whom no right-minded electrician would have wanted to fiddle, but by the electricity board, whom no right-minded electrician should really have wanted to fiddle either, but whom those electricians felt somehow happier about fiddling.

A little victory, then, for the underdog, is how one would have seen it. And the kind of victory which would have chimed loudly with the entrepreneurial vision of Derek Trotter, who had decided to build an entire career out of spotting such opportunities (albeit that he didn't tend to deliver them very successfully).

So when I saw that aspect of Del that John Sullivan was bringing to life in his scripts, I was able to think: yes, I know this person. And, of course, millions of viewers ending up feeling the same.

There was another aspect of Del that I found I could respond to at a personal level, in fact, and that was the way that, in so many of the comic scenarios John created for him, he's a man who has once again found himself socially out of his depth.

Now, as someone from a working-class background trying to make it in the world of acting, that was a predicament I could relate to. It's that 'comfortable in your own skin' thing again – that ability to move smoothly and certainly through the world, even when the going gets sophisticated. Some of us are born with that, and some of us acquire it, and some of us are always doing our best but just never quite get there.

I felt it quite keenly when we were making *Do Not Adjust Your Set*. Our little team got along extremely well and laughed a lot together and there was certainly no friction between us at any point. But Mike Palin, Terry Jones and Eric Idle were university mates. They were well read and very clever. My absent O levels weren't really cutting it in their company. They were completely at ease with each other and had their references, and I was definitely a bit of an outsider there.

Then there was that time at John Barron's place. In the mid-1970s I was in a touring production of *Charley's Aunt* with John, a wonderful actor – and I should say, incidentally, a person it was almost impossible to make corpse. Lord knows I tried during that run, but John was like granite.*

---

* History will relate that I got him just once – by, without warning, kind of treading my way up the inside of the floor-length dress I was wearing while the pair of us were walking downstage together in conversation, so that I actually seemed to be shrinking as we progressed. But that was the only time.

213

Anyway, I remember John inviting me to spend an evening at his house in Beauchamp Place in Knightsbridge. Very handy for Harrods, don't you know. Again, this was not the sort of area I'd spent much time in when I was growing up. From the distance of Lodge Lane, it might as well have been in another city, really.

For starters you needed to know that, despite strong appearances to the contrary in its spelling, it's pronounced 'Beecham Place'. So that was a potential social minefield right there – an opportunity to look gauche straight away by pronouncing it 'Bo-shamp' or 'Bew-chomp'. Ironically, even using the technically correct French style, 'Bo-shon', would have revealed you as a bit of an oik.

And I remember John greeting me at the door in a smoking jacket and I had clearly arrived just as he was on his way down to the wine cellar to bring up some bottles – because, yes, he had a wine cellar, with dozens of bottles of very lovely wine, all beautifully kept on racks.

So he took me down there, and while he was hunting out what he was looking for, I adopted an earnest and knowledgeable expression, as if hanging about in people's private wine cellars was something I did all the time. In truth, wine was something about which I knew absolutely nothing. I watched John pick out the bottles he needed and we headed back upstairs to the party.

Leonard Rossiter was there – John was in *The Fall and Rise of Reginald Perrin* with him – and Leonard, like John, knew about wine and could comfortably talk about things like 'palate' and 'nose' and 'bouquet', whereas I didn't have the first clue, really, what those words meant, apart from the obvious.

To my mortification, a wine-tasting now took place, with John and Leonard and some others who were there all taking sips of the wines that John had opened and making comparisons between them and discussing them. And, of course, this was a passage of the evening which essentially left me stranded on a desert island and listening to the seagulls.

'So, what do you think about *this* one?' John would say, pressing a glass on me.

What was I meant to say? 'Decent splash of plonk that, John.'

There was nothing I could do, really, except swill the wine around the glass in an experienced-looking manner, take some sips and make a series of what I hoped were the approximately correct noises.

'Hmm . . . ah . . . ooh . . . yes . . . hmm . . .'

I mean, I look back on it now and it was a Del Boy scene just waiting to be written.

But, of course, what Del had in those excruciating moments which I lacked was the ability to just barrel on through. Picture him at the opera that time, cheerfully oblivious to the decorum that he is noisily trampling over. Or think of him blasting away at the clay pigeons on the Duke of Maylebury's

estate with that borrowed bank robber's shotgun; or even
before that, tucking into a chicken leg and gesturing broadly
with it before absent-mindedly dumping the gnawed bone
on the fruit platter.

Very often, and especially when in full flow, Del wouldn't
really know a faux pas if it sneezed in his soup, frankly, and
indeed, he probably thinks faux pas is something to say to
someone when you're in agreement with them.

'Oh, *faux pas*, my friend, *faux pas*.'

Most of the time he's hilariously oblivious to the social
conventions he's leaving in absolute tatters behind him. All
the excruciation is being felt by others – well, that's their
problem.

And it's rather wonderful, that blithe self-assurance, isn't
it? I wish I'd had a little bit more of that. It would have made
that wine-tasting experience so much easier to get through.
And numerous other occasions since, too.

So, yes, I could bring things from my own experience to
the portrayal of Derek Trotter – but that didn't mean he
was entirely me, and it certainly didn't mean I wanted him
following me around wherever I went.

The fact was that Nick and I and the rest knew we wanted
to continue working beyond *Only Fools*. We had no problem
with that show becoming the biggest thing on our CVs – far
from it. How fantastic and how fortunate to be associated
with a show assuming that kind of scale. But we didn't want
it to be the *last* thing on our CVs, which, looking around

216

us, seemed to be a genuine threat with successful television comedies unless you played your cards very carefully.

People often ask me why I think *Only Fools* has persisted the way it has. And one reason, of course, is straightforwardly technological.

In the early 1980s, when *Only Fools* wasn't very old, we were in rehearsals one day and Lennard Pearce was talking about this newfangled device he'd been reading about – a video recorder. A VCR, they seemed to be calling them. You could record programmes off the telly onto video cassettes and watch them later. No longer would you need to be a slave to the TV schedules.

Imagine such a thing! Recording off the telly! No longer being in thrall to the pages of the *Radio Times*! The future was truly with us.

Lennard was asking Nick if he'd seen one and if he was going to get one. Nick said he thought they were a bit pricey. Which, of course, they were at the time: an arm, a leg and the other arm as well. A Sony VCR in 1982 would have set you back about £300 – which is the equivalent of around £1,000 in 2024 terms. A sizeable chunk.

But Lennard, it turned out, wasn't so much excited about owning a VCR and recording things to watch in his own time. He was seeing the bigger picture here, if you will forgive the pun.

'The thing is,' he said to Nick, 'what this means is, we're going to be around forever.'

217

It's hard to remember now just how transitory television programmes once seemed. If you missed them when they went out, that was it – you'd missed them. You wouldn't get another chance until the programme got repeated. It was only with the arrival of video that a television series became something you might keep and go back to. In due course, VHS gave way to DVD, and now there's the limitless library represented by the internet which means that nothing ever really goes away and everything is instantly available at every point.

But it was VHS that initially changed the way in which television shows were able to stick around in people's lives, and those of us involved with *Only Fools* were the first generation who really benefited from that.

However, you still needed to make a show that people wanted to tape, a show that people couldn't bear to miss. And the man behind that was, of course, John Sullivan, and the longevity of *Only Fools* is ultimately down to John's genius as a writer.

I often think about how John wrote alone. Very commonly, sitcom writers work in pairs – these days even in teams, on the American model. I've known some exceptions, of course: Ronnie Taylor, Roy Clarke, David Nobbs. But you think of Galton and Simpson, Muir and Norden, Croft and Perry, Clement and La Frenais, Esmonde and Larby, French and Saunders, Gervais and Merchant, Armstrong and Bain . . . The creators of our most enduring television comedies have tended to be partnerships.

All of those writers had someone else to bounce things off, someone to help them when things got sticky. Not John, though, who took on the burden of all that writing for *Only Fools*, and battled the deadlines and the pressure of delivering and redelivering a hugely popular show on his own. But perhaps that explains why what he produced was so individual, so singular. Certainly there were some set ideas at the time about what sitcom writing was, and then John came along writing in a new style, a style of his own – much more character-driven, shifting sitcom in the direction of comedy drama.

Here's an example of the difference. It comes from a moment when we were making series four.

I walked into the rehearsal room one day and, much to my surprise, found Buster playing the piano.

'I didn't know you were a piano player,' I said.

'I'm not really – I'm just killing time,' Buster replied.

To which, unable to help myself, I said, 'It sounds like you're killing the tune an' all.'

But if Buster was a pianist, it seemed like there was an opportunity to use that and create something in the show for Uncle Albert. I started nudging John to work in a moment for Albert at the piano. So that's why at one point you see Buster bashing away at the battered old pub instrument in the Nag's Head.

But what you don't see is Del, or anyone else, pulling the rug from under Buster with a caustic remark about the quality of his playing.

219

What you see instead is Trigger remarking, lugubriously, 'He's good, ain't he? I like that.'

And then, after a pause: 'I hope he don't do no more, though.'

I love that moment. How easy it would have been to detonate Albert's piano playing with a straightforward putdown – a line like my own when I found Buster in the rehearsal room. That would be the standard sitcom move.

But John gives the line to Trigger and has it start out as praise which then switches to the opposite, so that the laugh comes for Trigger as much as it comes for Albert and his dodgy playing. Touches like that are, I would say, the difference between John Sullivan and many other proponents of this art, and it's the consequence of being right inside your characters' heads at every stage of the writing.

And the results seem somehow timeless. Jerry Seinfeld – who wrote with Larry David, of course, another of the great partnerships – gave an interview recently in which he described the work of comedy writers and performers as being a bit like skiing. Specifically he seemed to be thinking about those competitions where people fling themselves down the mountain between plastic gates.

'Culture – the gates are moving,' Seinfeld said. 'Your job is to be agile and clever enough that, wherever they put the gates, I'm going to make the gate.'

Well, I've only been on a skiing holiday once in my life – at the invitation of some friends, back in the 1970s, in Switzerland where, entirely naive about these things, I took to the slopes in a pair of unsuitable cotton trousers and then had to leave important parts of myself to thaw on the radiator for about three and a half weeks afterwards.

But, even in my state of Alpine inexperience, I think I understand the point Seinfeld is making there.*

Ideas about what's funny change, obviously. And very often we develop our strongest attachments to the things we found funny when we were younger – the programmes from *our* times, *our* comedy. We can all be quite protective in this area – maybe even competitively so.

I suppose you might say that comedy is no different from pop music in that respect. 'My generation's pop music was better than your generation's pop music.' People have been saying that to each other since pop music was invented.

And seeing as we're on the subject, my generation's pop music was the Beatles, so my generation's pop music *was* better than your generation's pop music and I'm right, simple as that. End of argument.

Seriously, though, here's where I know I've been exceptionally lucky. *Only Fools* has proved itself to be not just funny but lastingly funny. Even now it continues to feature in the lists of the UK's favourite ever comedies – frequently

---

* 'Do you have salopettes?' my rather posh hosts had asked me on that occasion. 'Well, funnily enough, I did once,' I replied, 'around about the same time I had tender perennials. But the same ointment seemed to do for both.'

221

at the top of the pile and always up there with *Fawlty Towers*, *Blackadder* and *The Office* as the shows that people remember most fondly and just can't stop laughing at.

I know that many of the people who loved *Only Fools* at the time still love it now. I know this because they are constantly coming up and telling me so. Sometimes, if these conversations are taking place at the annual *Only Fools and Horses* convention, they will tell me so while dressed in full-length chandelier costumes to further make the point.* I also know from those conversations that a whole lot of other, younger people have discovered the show since and found that it makes them laugh, too.

And yet it's now been four decades and counting since the programme first entered the nation's living rooms. We've had the time to outgrow quite a lot of things in that time: compact discs, diesel car engines, slimline *Sunday Telegraph* Gardener's Diaries . . .

I mean, Jane Fonda-style workout leggings were all the rage when *Only Fools* was initially in its pomp, but I haven't worn mine in ages now – not even during my post-operation static-bike workouts.

Yet *Only Fools* rolls on, somehow immune to these shifts

---

* 'There's a girl here who's come as a chandelier,' I was told at the 2023 convention – leading me to expect some kind of hat. But no. This was a floor-length, full-body chandelier outfit, hung with a copious quantity of glass candles. To carry off something like that with style takes some chutzpah. My own metaphorical hat was off to her.

of fad and fashion. You're quite hard-pressed, in fact, to find a joke in it that feels date-stamped. I've given this some thought and there's just one laugh line that I've managed to isolate which could currently be felt to be sitting uncomfortably below time's unsparing axe.

It's in 'The Jolly Boys' Outing' when Del is playing Trivial Pursuit with Cassandra's boss, Stephen – exactly one of those socially mismatched scenarios we've been talking about, with the yuppie Stephen being contemptuous of Del, who barely even notices, really, believing he and Stephen, as young, thrusting men of business, to be entirely sympatico.

So up comes Del's question, accompanied by gloating from Stephen about how easy it is: 'What is the name for a female swan?'

The answer is a 'pen' – which you might not have known any more than Del does, but you'd have presumably picked up a clue when Rodney takes a pen from his jacket and starts tapping it on his teeth and waving it helpfully in Del's direction.

Finally the penny drops.

'Got it!' says Del. 'It's a Bic.'

Never mind the word 'plonker': for how much longer will the word 'Bic' automatically mean 'pen' for younger generations, who may actually be struggling to recognise the word 'pen' not too far from now, the way things are going.

So, this time next year . . . well, maybe nobody's finding that funny.

I'm racking my brains, though, to think of other gags in the scripts that are potentially threatened with extinction, and I'm coming up blank. You can't be entirely confident, of course. But it does seem to me that the number of endangered jokes in *Only Fools* looks vanishingly small.

What I'm saying is, the show has long outlived the period in which it was made, and it has slipped and dodged through the obstacles that life has thrown at it. We shoved it down the mountain, you might say, and, over the last forty-plus years, so far it hasn't significantly clattered into any of those gates that Seinfeld talked about.

Nor has it, like so many downhill skiers before it, gone head-over-backside on the icy slope and ended up spatchcocked on the plastic fencing. Which might have been appropriate, in some ways, for a programme containing characters like Del and Rodney, but which, in the bigger picture, would have been a shame for all involved.

Two things to say about that, though. Firstly, none of us envisaged any of this at the time. OK, we might have dimly worked out, with the help of Lennard, that the arrival in the world of the video recorder would give us a chance to hang around a little longer than television programmes had habitually done.

But it was a long leap from that to the idea of remaining popular for forty years and none of us, I can assure you, in breaks between filming or over a curry after a day's shooting, was sitting back from the table and saying: 'Solid day's work, everyone. I reckon people will still be talking about what we achieved today in four decades' time, you see if I'm wrong.'

Had anybody among our number come out with a line like that, they would have been greeted with hoots of derision and maybe also a pelting with bits of poppadom. Forty years? Are you having a laugh?

More than that, none of us had any control over what became of the show in the long term, either. That's simply not possible. You put these programmes out there in the hope that they're going to land with people, first and fore-most. The hope that time might be kind to them is a lot further down your wish list, if it even appears there at all. And both those things – whether it lands with people, whether time is eventually kind to it – are entirely out of your hands.

Here's a thought, too: for all the dreams and longings mentioned elsewhere in this chapter, would any film role I might have found have possibly had the lastingly deep impact Derek Trotter has had? It's hard to imagine so, isn't it?

He who dares, wins, then. Hollywood? Pah!

CHAPTER SIX

Of dodgy jives, wonky baskets and this great nation of tinkerers

A nd then finally it came – an end to the post-pandemic drought. Just when I had started to think that it was all over, and that never again would this poor player be called upon to strut and fret his hour upon the nation's television screens – or to strut and fret his half-hour, if that was the format, or his forty-five minutes or whatever – something showed up. And not just a meeting this time. An actual offer of actual work.

And I had *Strictly Come Dancing* to thank for it.

No, I wasn't invited to compete on the show, although I can understand you leaping to that conclusion. So far my exquisitely well-formed paso doble, though greatly admired down the years by all who have witnessed it, has for some reason failed to attract the attention of the *Strictly* selectors.

Actually, in all seriousness, I was asked to do a dance

for the 2012 Christmas special, but I turned it down for a number of reasons. Mainly two left feet. Ah well. It was the viewing public's loss, I'm sure.

But Jay Blades had been picked – and that, as unlikely as it may seem, was the original kink of fate, if I may put it that way, that would ultimately lead to me finding my way back into a television series in 2024.

Fate's aforementioned kink did its kinking in 2021, when the host of *The Repair Shop* was asked to join the likes of Moira Stuart and Adrian Chiles in the annual one-off *Strictly Come Dancing* contest for broadcast on Christmas Day.

Moreover, it was relayed to me beforehand by the show's producers that Jay wanted to use his appearance to pay homage to one of his favourite television shows. He was intending to take the closing theme music from *Only Fools* – 'Hooky Street', John Sullivan's song about half-price cracked ice, gold chains, wosnames, etc. – and, in the character of Derek Trotter, or at least in some of Derek Trotter's clothing, Jay was going to perform a jive to it.

My first reaction was: he's possibly not quite right in the head.

My second reaction was: I should definitely agree to send him a message of encouragement, via video, that the show can use on the night.

I mean, dancing to 'Hooky Street'? Dressed as Del Boy? This was going to be either the world's biggest ever victory over the odds, or the greatest disaster in the history of televised pro-celebrity ballroom dancing since Ann Widdecombe did the samba.

And either way I was desperate to see it.*

Of course, all this was going on while the pandemic was still spoiling our lives and when film crews were being discouraged from floating around the country and recording messages of support for celebrity dancers in advance of their appearance on Christmas specials unless it was absolutely necessary.

So my performance-enhancing video clip had to be shot at home in private by a film crew of one – Gill with her iPhone. As such, you will appreciate, it was filmed in accordance with the very highest production values and sparing neither expense nor effort. Why, I went all the way upstairs to dig out a red sweater, a flat cap and a brown leather jacket. And then I went all the way downstairs again.

And then I stood against a plain backdrop in the form of a wall in our house, and I looked directly into the lens of Gill's phone and delivered some words of inspiration, many long hours in the composing, which drew deeply on the proven techniques of the very best motivational psychologists.

* Ann Widdecombe's samba took place on *Strictly* in 2010, in Blackpool, in the arms of Anton Du Beke, and the world still reels. Craig Revel-Horwood described the politician's dance as 'overwhelmingly awful' and Len Goodman felt obliged to state: 'It's like haemorrhoids – they keep coming back more painful than ever.' The dance earned 13 points out of 40 which, for non-aficionados of *Strictly*, is . . . not good.

I won't duplicate those words in full here, for fear of having the details of my style scrutinised and copied by pale imitators. But the vital essence of this soaring piece of rhetoric could be boiled down to four words:

'Go on, my son.'

Reviewing this work of art before we sent it off, I felt the surge of satisfaction that only arises from a job well done and a dancer well encouraged. I imagine Mel Gibson felt much the same when he reviewed the final cut of the 'Freedom' speech scene in *Braveheart*.

Moreover, my videoed vote of confidence would be shown to Jay for the first time in that critical moment when he went upstairs after the performance to receive his scores. At that precise point, then, he would know that he had the backing and the blessing of Del's representative here on Earth, and that knowledge would surely cause him to feel that the trophy was as good as in the bag. (He was in tears, actually.)

Frankly, I found it hard to imagine how he could possibly lose from there.

But, of course, I had never seen Jay dance.

Now, Jay was not alone out there on the dance floor. He had the potentially reassuring company of one of *Strictly*'s team of certified professionals, Luba Mushtuk – although once the performance got going, it occurred to me to wonder whether it might be more appropriate to think of her less as a partner, in this particular context, and more as a carer.

Either way, Jay and Luba danced together to John's song,

as promised, and in the vicinity of a fruit and veg stall, a mock-up of the outside of the Nag's Head and a yellow Reliant Regal.

Well, I say 'danced' . . . In Jay's case, it was more of a hopscotch, really, than a dance. Jokes about my paso doble notwithstanding, I'll admit I'm no expert on ballroom's finer points, and even on the very best of days cannot be relied upon to know one end of my cha-cha from the other.

But I know what a wardrobe falling down the stairs looks like, and that was my overall impression of Jay's jive.

Harsh? OK, possibly a little bit . . . But I had certainly seen big pieces of wooden furniture move more smoothly than Jay did in the routine's trickier moments.

Watching all this unfold that Christmas from my armchair at home, and oblivious to what it would eventually portend, I shook my head wisely and reached forward to dip my hand into the ever-open Quality Street tin.

'Stick to mending things, matey,' I told the screen.

As it turned out, the actual judges, who we must assume know what they're talking about, didn't object as strongly as I imagined they would to the gruesome scene they had just witnessed. Indeed, they awarded Jay a total mark of 34 out of 40, which even allowing for the generous, giving spirit that tends as a matter of course to be in the air around the festive season, wasn't too shabby.

Naturally, from this distance in history and with the benefit of hindsight, I bow to their greater authority.

It wasn't enough to clinch the prize for Jay, though. That went to the singer Anne-Marie who did a cha-cha with no *Only Fools* associations whatsoever and got full marks for it.

Lesson for future participants there, maybe: if you want to travel the road to ballroom glory on a Christmas *Strictly*, avoid taking Derek Trotter with you. I would have thought it was obvious, but clearly you never know.

Second lesson for ballroom glory seekers: avoid taking Jay Blades with you also. But, again, that's probably transparent at this stage.

Anyway, soon after this, Jay got in touch to thank me for my little video and, by way of return, invited me and Gill down to West Sussex to have a look around the barn where he and his team film *The Repair Shop*.

We're both big admirers of that show. Indeed, it's one of the shows Gill and I regularly watch together with completely equal enthusiasm on both sides. This sets it apart from, say, *MasterChef*, which I would suggest skews more towards Gill on the enthusiasm side, and *Police Interceptors*, which skews more towards me. But on such carefully negotiated compromises, of course, is a happy marriage founded.

Anyway, *The Repair Shop* is all right by both of us, and we happily accepted the invitation to see where it all takes place.

Which is how come, one sunny day, I found myself looking

up for the first time at the smiling, six-foot-three figure of Jay Blades from directly below it, and hearing myself say, by way of greeting: 'Blimey, you don't get any shorter, do you?'

As we toured the barn and met all the experts and specialist repairers and watched everyone very happily going about their business, it was immediately apparent that Jay and I were going to rub along well. That was partly because the man is a ball of friendly energy and it's impossible not to warm to that and be drawn along by him.

Wasn't it the writer Terry Pratchett who eventually cracked the secret of perpetual motion, which had eluded scientists since the dawn of time? And didn't he do it by pointing out that cats always land on their feet, and that toast always lands butter-side down? So therefore, if you strap a piece of buttered toast, butter upwards, to the back of a cat and drop it . . . eureka, you've created perpetual motion.

Well, in theory.

Anyway, I've got a simpler suggestion for the scientists: Jay Blades. That's your answer right there. That man is perpetual motion personified – constantly on the move, constantly in demand, constantly working. I see a lot of my younger self in that determination of Jay's to keep the diary full. I see quite a bit of my older self, too, if I'm being honest.

In fact, Jay and I come from the same place on a lot of things. And I don't just mean London, the city of our birth – though there is that.

Jay is someone who has made his way up from not much, who has overcome setbacks and climbed over barriers that were in his path, and done something extraordinary with his life through his own hard graft and determination. If you want to know more about Jay's story, you should read his book, if you haven't already.*

Now, I'm not suggesting for a moment that I had it anywhere near as hard as Jay did, growing up. But, like him, I know what it is to be working class, to find yourself handed very little in the way of advantages, and to feel somehow automatically discouraged as a consequence of your circumstances.

So there was very quickly a connection between us because, yes, here we were, two faces off the television, but we both knew about what's involved in trying to get to where you want to be when you come from a background where not much is expected of you. And, to use Jay's lovely phrase: 'Real recognises real.'

And then there's the ethos of *The Repair Shop*. One of Jay's themes is the value of fixing things up rather than chucking them away – choosing restoration over replacement. And here I'm right on board, and have been all my life. The phrase 'make-do and mend' was instilled in my generation.

---

* *Making It: How Love, Kindness and Community Helped Me Repair My Life* by Jay Blades. I'm not on a commission here, but maybe I ought to be . . .

It appeared on government posters in London during the war as part of the campaign to get people to save on precious resources by repairing their clothes, so I literally grew up staring at that motto. In a time of rationing, you couldn't help but learn lessons about the importance of economising.* It instilled in me an aversion to waste, not to mention a habit of turning off the lights when I left a room. For quite a long time you could come across as a bit fuddy-duddy for insisting that that was important – but less so nowadays, I notice. We increasingly understand that the resources we've been taking for granted are actually finite, that they need preserving, and recycling has become a modern-day mission.

I knew if I waited long enough I'd be fashionable.

I told Jay about saving up for ages, back in my late teens, to buy a second-hand BSA B31 motorbike – the dream, the vehicle that would set me free!

And, quite literally while riding the bike home from the seller's house, and feeling about as thrilled with myself as I had ever felt, I suddenly started hearing a rhythmical knocking noise of a highly discouraging nature coming from underneath me.

I got off and crouched down to have a look and discovered that the frame of my lovely motorbike had obviously at some

---

* Rationing continued well after the end of the war in 1945. Petrol rationing didn't end until 1950, when I was ten. Sugar and confectionery rationing ended three years after that in 1953, and meat rationing in 1954.

235

point in its life snapped in half and had been cheaply welded back together. And that weld had now come apart, leaving the engine flapping about like washing in a breeze.

Naturally I pushed this lame item straight back to the seller's house to get an instant refund with no questions asked, and to receive a sincere apology on his part for trying it on big time.

So much for that.

'Sorry, mate. Sold as seen.'

Well, you find out about repair work very quickly when something like that happens to you. I couldn't afford to take that ruptured bike to the garage, so I had to work out how to fix it up myself. Which I did. And then that self-reliance stays with you.

Jay related to that – but then I knew he would. This is someone who once built himself a wardrobe for his bedroom, there being no money around for such a thing, using old milk crates and a sawn-off broomstick for a rail.

There's something else we both believe in, which is the value of tinkering and making things, not just from the economic point of view, but for its own sake. It's another version of that saying I set so much store by: that it's the journey, not the arrival. Of course, it's satisfying to finish a project, to sit back from it and take pleasure in what you've done. But the real joy lies in getting absorbed by the process, by the craft itself. That's where investing your energy really gets its reward – in the moment rather than in the anticipation. It's true of hobbies, and it's equally true of work, in my experience.

It's Jay's belief that while some people have intelligent minds, and get readily commended for them, other people have intelligent hands, and that the people with intelligent hands don't necessarily get the respect or the encouragement they deserve. He's doing his best to change that attitude, and I'm with him all the way on that.

There's also a worry, which again we share, that manual skills in general are on the slide, and that some of them are going to slide away from us for good if we're not careful, if we don't make sure to look after them and shine a light on them when we can.

This is the digital age, after all. We're growing accustomed to a world where practically everything comes to us via the mobile phone. It's all on there, all provided for us: music, television, games, shopping . . .

All of which can be fantastically convenient, of course. But what then happens to using your hands and your imagination to make something? How are people going to come to know the pleasure and value of creating things when they can just pick up their phone and occupy themselves with that instead? It sounds like a contradiction in terms, but it's true: when everything is instantly available, people end up missing out.

Anyway, I took along to that meeting with Jay a video of Marvo the Mystic, the coin-operated machine that I restored at home with Brian Cosgrove, my great film-making friend from Cosgrove Animations. Of all the things I've built in my workshop at home, it's the restoration job I'm most proud of.

So we talked about that, and then I told him about the five-inch gauge railway I've built in my garden, and the two steam engines I run on it, which I put together from kits.

And then I told him about my rocket-building projects and how, on A *Touch of Frost*, I would often mark the end of filming by going out with the cast and launching a home-built rocket, just for the hell of it. Other people would bring in cakes; I would bring in rockets. It's a sure-fire way to make your party go with a bang.

The conversations we had in Sussex that day planted something in Jay's mind, and he began talking about finding a way to bring our mutual enthusiasm together on the telly. And eventually, out of all that, came *David and Jay's Touring Toolshed*, the idea being to take something of the spirit of *The Repair Shop* out on the road – to travel round the UK with a shed full of tools, parking up at county fairs, steam rallies, air shows, you name it, meeting people who roll up their sleeves and make and mend things, and hooking them up with experts for additional help if they needed it.

The BBC commissioned the series from Jay's production company, Hungry Jay Media, and we filmed the shows in the middle of 2023, dodging the rain showers of a typical British summer and making fifteen half-hour episodes from a voyage which took us all over the country, from Worcestershire to Cheshire to Cullen on the coast of Banffshire in Scotland.

We ended up seeing all sorts – from the basket weaver who was having problems with wonky baskets, to the model-maker who was struggling with the finer details of making the head move convincingly on her latest animated masterpiece.

Incidentally, it was while we were filming the basket-weaving segment that I made the mortifying mistake of referring to the raw material for that craft as 'twigs'.

We don't call them 'twigs', as I now most certainly know. We call them 'wands'. Do bear that in mind and save yourself some embarrassment the next time you're discussing wonky baskets with a basket weaver.

Much in evidence on our travels were members of what I like to think of as the British Eccentrics Society – the creators of home-made robots, the people from the Sack-field Flying Club who spend their leisure time making hot-air balloons, the people who are active on the competitive chain-sawing circuit, the members of a women's rowing team who have built their own boat from scratch, the lawnmower racers who have adapted their mowers to travel at speeds of up to 50mph, and whom I'd love to see cut my grass. They'd have the job done and dusted before they'd even started.

And then there were the 'yarn bombers' – the 170-strong society of knitters, crochet workers and soft-toy makers who go by the name of the Toppers of Northwich, who very sweetly presented me with a felt Danger Mouse and who were busy, when we visited, knitting pineapples for the Northwich Pina Colada Festival.

A Pina Colada Festival? In Northwich? Yes, because Rupert Holmes, who wrote and recorded that 1979 hit 'The Pina Colada Song' was born in Northwich.

But you knew that.*

One day, to my particular delight, the great-niece of the legendary Tony Hancock arrived with a huge teddy bear that Hancock had brought back from Hong Kong in the sixties, on an aeroplane, in its own seat. There are photographs of Hancock conducting interviews while sat at home in this bear's lap, for all the world as if it were a giant sofa. Inevitably, the bear was now showing signs of sixty years of wear and tear, including one greatly diminished ear. So we had it put right, with the help of an expert upholsterer, and it went home good as new.

I never worked with Tony Hancock, and only wish that I had. But at least I can now say that I've worked with his ornamental bear.

And because the spirit of Derek Trotter is never far away when I'm around, at one point I found myself face-to-face with a man who at one time in his life had owned fifty-two Reliant three-wheelers, Regals and Robins in all forms and colours, but had now slimmed his collection down to what

---

* The official title of that Rupert Holmes song is 'Escape (The Pina Colada Song)'. But you knew that too.

he reckoned was a far more manageable twenty. I asked him why he loved them so much and he replied that, until you'd driven one, you just couldn't know the deeply appealing nature of the vehicle.

I had to point out at that juncture that I *had* driven one – several, in fact – and that I was still mystified about what the appeal was, remembering in particular how the search for gears in that terrible old banger that I was obliged to handle on the various sets of *Only Fools* could exhaust whole hours. Indeed, I'm still to this very day not entirely sure that, in seven series of playing Derek Trotter, I ever found fourth.

But our man with the Reliant collection was not to be dissuaded from his love. A passion is a passion, and ours is not to reason why.

And then there was the man from Cullen who started making a tapestry during lockdown, just to fill some time, and didn't stop until it was a record-shattering 250 feet long. That made me feel a bit better about my expanding set of riding-boot lamps and my home-threatening collection of wooden automata.

There's a narrative that has taken hold in recent years, that the country is broken in many ways, that lots of things don't work properly any more, that things we were once able to take for granted as we went about our everyday lives have been neglected and allowed to go to pot. And it's not based on nothing, that narrative.

But what was so positive and invigorating about going

around the UK with Jay and the Touring Toolshed was the way it caused you to set that narrative aside and see something else that was true – namely that we're still a nation of tinkerers, and that creativity and invention are still out there and thriving. And you barely need to scratch the surface to find them.

*   *   *

I quite fancied travelling between locations for *Touring Toolshed* by my favourite mode of transport, the helicopter. I used my helicopter on many work and research projects. It was a very useful tool to get me, for example, to many a country house deep in the wilds of the countryside while investigating underground tunnels and 'priest holes' for a possible documentary series which I'm still very hopeful of getting commissioned. I reckoned there would be some lovely flying to be done between those places we were visiting, weather permitting. But there were two good reasons why that didn't happen.

Firstly, the BBC and Jay's production company, though happy to stump up for the odd bacon roll here and there, would have baulked at running to the expense of laying on a helicopter for the exclusive use of the presenters – and fair enough, I suppose.

Secondly, I couldn't use my own helicopter because my solo-piloting days had recently come to an end.

Yes, with extreme reluctance, I had hung up my flying jacket. It was a moment for rueful reflection, I can't deny. As I've mentioned before, I had been quietly going for a place in the Guinness World Records: oldest solo-pilot helicopter flight.

That record has been held since 2017 by a British gentleman named David Marks, who was eighty-seven and forty days when he set it. I was gunning for his title, and closing in on him fast. But I didn't get there.

Ah well. I made it into my eighties, at least, and put getting on for 650 hours of flying in my logbook, all told. That's a decent spell in the cockpit and one I know I can be pleased with.

But the fact is, you need your hips, legs and knees to be in pretty tip-top condition for helicopter flying. Also your arms and shoulders. It's rather like playing a drum kit in that regard, although the consequences of getting out of time during the second verse are quite a bit graver. Unless, perhaps, you're Keith Moon, my unpredictable doppelgänger, whom we mentioned earlier.

Anyway, I realised I was getting increasingly uncomfortable up there in the air. Having to push the physical part of the task was taking some of the joy out of it. Clearly it was time to step away while I was still capable of stepping.

So I landed for the last time, departed the cockpit with all the dignity I could muster, and put the helicopter up for sale.

No, not on eBay, in case that's what you were thinking. I

sold it (one careful owner, immaculate condition, full service history) to someone at the airfield I used to visit. I felt a bit like somebody reluctantly getting rid of a sports car because they can't get down low enough to climb into it without groaning. But it had to happen eventually. The helicopter now lives near Shoreham on the south coast which at least means that I can drop in and see it when I'm down that way visiting my sister.

People used to ask me, 'Why did you learn to fly a helicopter?' And it may sound masochistic, but the honest answer was, because I knew it was going to be difficult. Helicopters are pretty widely agreed to be the hardest things in the world to fly.

OK, if we're going to be pedantic, the lunar lander with which the Apollo crews took themselves down to the surface of the moon, was probably harder – a pretty tricky beast to control. But when I was scouting around for lessons, the lunar lander didn't seem to be an option for the weekend learner, and wouldn't have been particularly handy for my purposes anyway. So a helicopter it was.

'Why not fly a plane?' people would say. And I did a little bit of that, and very much enjoyed it. But, of course, you can't get planes in and out of posh country houses the way you can helicopters.

OK, a Harrier jump jet is quite manoeuvrable. But they look askance at you if you try and bring one of those down at a hotel or a filming location. And though it's a sensational piece of engineering, it's not really a tool for the business traveller in quite the way that a helicopter is.

And also, pilots won't like me for saying so, but planes fly themselves; or, at any rate, they have wings so they will naturally glide through the air. However, you have a much better fighting chance if you happen to be in a helicopter and its engines fail. A helicopter pilot is trained to enter auto-rotation, where you use the air travelling through the blades to maintain your lift and then descend to the ground in, of course, much tighter spaces than a fixed wing could.

Anyway, I chose helicopters for the sheer challenge of it, in order to stretch myself. Quite often in life, you'll hear that little voice in your head saying, 'Ooh, I don't know . . . I'm not sure someone like me could handle something like that.' And sometimes it's good to ignore that voice and give it a go anyway. If you don't try, after all, you never find out. And maybe more often than you think, that little voice will turn out to have been wrong all along, as little voices in your head so frequently are.

I certainly never came to regret ignoring the voice in this case. Gliding, where I started out on my flying journey, was thrilling, definitely – and I'll never forget the feeling of taking a glider up on my own for the first time, and doing a circuit without an instructor: the cockpit getting closed over my head, the anxious wait on the ground to get winched into the air, the absolute solitude, the silence up there, with just the wind going past the canopy, and the elation of bringing it down at the end and feeling the skid touch the ground, and thinking, 'I did it! I flew solo!'

But taking a helicopter up alone for my maiden solo flight and bringing it home again topped all of that for a sense of achievement, and continued to do so every time I flew. Of course, I wrestled in my conscience with the fuel consumption of such a machine, but I used it as sparingly as I could and feel confident that helicopter manufacturers will continue to make huge advances in this regard, just as we're doing with cars and other vehicles. If I could have flown on vegetable oil, I would have done.

I only had one truly frightening moment, in all those hours in the air. That was while heading with my friend Rod Brown to a meeting at a hotel in the countryside. I was bringing the helicopter down, as prearranged, towards a nearby patch of open land, when we were suddenly buffeted by a huge gust of wind which knocked the helicopter sideways and sent it through a 360-degree spin.

For a fleeting second, I thought the tail rotor had gone, which is the biggest nightmare in the book of helicopter nightmares. There's very little taking back control if that happens. You're pretty much in the hands of gravity from that moment on. When I realised, with a flood of relief, that the tail rotor was still with us, I set us straight again. And then I erred entirely on the side of caution. Rather than reattempt the landing, I simply flew us up and away.

Lunch meeting postponed, which was a shame. But better safe and hungry than sorry.

I think I was a good, safe pilot in general – instinctively cautious, certainly risk-averse. Unlike David Tomlinson, another actor-pilot, whom you might remember I mentioned earlier in relation to his appearances in the movies of *Mary Poppins* and *Bedknobs and Broomsticks*, and also that Wombles film I voiced. David had learned to fly during the war and his idea of weekend fun was doing aerobatics in a Tiger Moth aeroplane, flipping and spinning for pleasure.

One time he flipped and spun so enthusiastically that he lost consciousness and crashed in some woodland just behind his back garden. That he survived and lived to a grand old age is probably testament to his enormous luck on that occasion, and the fact that he went easy on the flying afterwards.

Incidentally, once asked to say what he would like his epitaph to be, David thought about it for a while and then said: 'Actor of genius, irresistible to women.' I might borrow that.

Anyway, flying that helicopter was a big part of my life. It was a lot of fun, obviously, but also just the most satisfying accomplishment. Some people have the piano, and some people have oil painting. And some people, as I discovered on *Touring Toolshed* have knitting pineapples. But I had the helicopter. And it's over now, but I'll always be proud that I can call myself a qualified helicopter pilot.

*   *   *

247

You'll be wondering, I'm sure, how it worked out for Jay and me on the set of *Touring Toolshed*, and which of us had the biggest trailer.

Well, I can answer that question very swiftly for you: neither of us had the biggest trailer because there weren't any trailers. Although the budget for this major, nationally broadcast production ran to a toolshed, it didn't run to any on-location dressing rooms.

Ah, the days of the luxury motorhome! I remember them well. Because it's not just movie stars who get to hold their hands to their brows and say, 'I'll be in my trailer if you need me.' Some of us TV stars get to say that as well, you know.

Things really revved up in that department when I went over to ITV. I'd been used to the BBC-funded, nicotine-stained caravan I shared with Nick on *Only Fools*.

'I'll be in my nicotine-stained caravan if you need me.'

It doesn't have the same ring, somehow.

But when ITV offered me some work, I was suddenly in the world of commercial television, where the budgets available for pampering the talent were clearly more generous.

Certainly the facilities that were made available to me on the set for *The Darling Buds of May* were a definite step up. I should be clear, however, that I didn't request that this should be the case. I didn't have my agent call up in advance and say, 'By the way, David's going to need a deluxe motorhome, an unlimited supply of kiwi fruit, ready-peeled, and a basket for his chihuahua.'

248

Look, I'd come from *Only Fools*, so my expectations were actually zero. Also, I'm not terribly fond of kiwi fruit. And I don't have a chihuahua.*

But even without me making any special requests, I felt I had lucked out. The trailer made available to me down there in Kent was a far smarter affair than the old caravan, with, it seemed, many fewer miles on the clock and seats which hadn't been sat on so long and so hard that they no longer had any stuffing.

And it definitely seemed to have staged far fewer smoking contests. Plus, get this: it was actually somewhere that was quite nice to sit in for a while. What a radical idea. I remember thinking, 'I could get used to this.'

And as for the one after that, on *A Touch of Frost* . . . blimey.

I still remember the member of the production staff saying, 'Mr Jason, I'll show you to your trailer,' and then leading me to this shiny monster, roughly on the scale of an adult blue whale. I thought, 'You are joking . . .' It was gargantuan.

---

* I have Tuffy, who is a lazy Labrador, and Bella, who is a mix of several things, including some Bedlington and some Boston terrier but not including, to the best of my knowledge, any chihuahua. Incidentally, while you're down here, both of these dogs are available on a professional basis for dropped-food clearance, either individually or as a team, at extremely reasonable prices to be negotiated, depending on the scale of the clearance, distance from me in Buckinghamshire, etc. Apply using one of the blank pages that will almost certainly be hanging around at the back of this book.

And from inside it seemed even bigger. I reckon I'd been in smaller sports halls. In fact, if they had called an election, that trailer would have been its own constituency: David Jason's Caravan West.

What can I say? Glorious times.

'I'll be in my deluxe motorhome if you need me. And so, quite possibly, will be thirty-five other people, for all that I'll even notice them, given the length of the thing.'

No such star treatment on *Touring Toolshed*, though. At each of the locations we had a little fenced-off area with, if we were lucky, a couple of pop-up tents quickly thrown up by the production staff for everybody to use. Somewhere in this zone, Jay and I each had a canvas chair with our names on which we could plonk ourselves down on when we needed to. Of course, I'd come back and find Jay deliberately sitting in mine to wind me up. Or I'd deliberately sit in *his* to wind *him* up. But those personalised canvas chairs were the full extent of our cosseting.

'I'll be on my personalised canvas chair if you need me.'

Nobody's saying that.

As for the catering truck . . . well, there was no catering truck. Or no *official* catering truck. But most of the time we were at shows and fairs, so there were *multiple* catering trucks right on our doorstep – or at least right where our doorstep would have been if we'd had a trailer with a doorstep.

Happy days! Come lunchtime, orders would be taken and one of the crew would do a run to whatever stalls happened to be in the vicinity: hot dogs, pulled pork baps, a sausage-and-onion roll with a cup of tea, doughnuts . . . We knew how to live.

In all seriousness, I loved the whole experience from start to finish – loved being with the crew on the locations, loved meeting the people who came to the Toolshed to show us the products of their labours, and (I can say this openly here, because he's not around to hear it) loved being with Jay.

I'd not done very much, really, in the way of unscripted television before this, and Jay hadn't done very much in the way of comedy, so the two of us were learning from each other every day. And what I especially loved doing was devising the joke sequences and daft bits of business for us to get up to between the main action of the show.

I found myself reflecting how much of my working life has been spent crafting gags – making silly little unscripted moments work to create a laugh where there wasn't one before.

Like, for instance, figuring out how much milk you need to have in a milk bottle so that when your character goes to tip some milk into his mug of tea, it overshoots and slops onto the table in just the right quantity and at just the right distance from the mug to be properly funny. You'd be surprised how long you can spend experimenting with different milk levels in the bottle until you arrive at the optimum comic sloppage – the tipping point, as it were.

You'd probably be surprised, too, to learn how much time can be absorbed by working out the best way to get a remote-controlled robot with a wand in its hand to jab someone in the backside. That one was on *Still Open All Hours* – a moment in which Leroy, Granville's son and his poor, exhausted assistant in the corner shop, played by James Baxter, dozes off on the job and gets rudely awakened, in the manner described, by his tyrannical father, played by me.

You catch yourself at such times, half an hour into devising the best angle of approach for the robot and the optimum position for the victim to adopt so that his backside best presents itself to the robot's advances, and you marvel at what goes by the name of work in the world that you've landed up in.

Or here's one I remember from when I was in the theatre, in a production of *The Norman Conquests*, the trilogy of Alan Ayckbourn comedies. And my character, Norman, is drunk and trying to put a record on the spindle of a record player and, for a little while, failing hopelessly, much to his own inebriated confusion.

And that in itself was a funny enough sequence to perform. But it needed a clinching moment or else it kind of went nowhere. So I developed a little bit for the end of it where Norman holds the record up to the light, squints at it, and then blows hard, as if to unblock the hole in the record's middle. And after that little fix, the record goes on.

That one took a lot of thinking about and planning, and

then some further fine-tuning in front of the audience – where, I don't mind telling you, it eventually earned a huge laugh. So I guess it paid off.

But what can I tell you? Some of us are out there trying to solve the world's problems; some of us are out there trying to plot the funniest way for a drunk person to work out how to put on a record.

Being able to observe Ron Moody at work in the theatre was an enormously influential experience for me in this area – the way he went beyond the script to work on the audience, constantly looking for ways to draw them out of themselves and filling the room with laughter and energy. I watched him go to work, night after night, and thought: I would really love to have the courage and the ability to do that.

This was back in the 1960s, when I got one of my earliest breaks with a part in a production of *Peter Pan* where Ron was playing Captain Hook. For the first time I found myself near the West End in a well-funded show, with great sets and props, and acting alongside some established actors who had climbed through the ranks to the very top of their trade – not just Ron, but Julia Lockwood and Leslie Sarony. I was just an apprentice by comparison with these master craftspeople and it was a very formative few weeks.

But it was Ron who I was especially mesmerised by. If you read his autobiography you will learn that he was forever, especially in his early years as an actor but also beyond that, throwing in improvised bits and pieces and jokey additions to the lines that had been written for him. Directors don't always approve of that kind of thing, of course. And writers *really* don't approve of it.

But Ron took it further. Sometimes he even made his own props and adapted his own costumes. In one revue show he was in, he started coming out in a battered cloche hat that he had either borrowed or stolen from his mum. He had sewn big, stupid earflaps to this hat and then tied those earflaps to the end of a long-stemmed pipe which was clenched between his teeth.

Every time he took the pipe from his mouth, the earflaps shot up, and every time he put the pipe back in, the earflaps dropped again. On top of this, he started talking in a thick German accent. Nobody involved in the production could remember asking him to do any of this, or being consulted by him regarding whether it was OK or not.

And the point of it all – the stupid hat, the unexplained accent? There was no point: Ron just thought it was funny.

Now, there's no question that some of what Ron got up to in these areas will have earned him the exasperation – and sometimes probably the fury – of his directors. It can't have been easy for his fellow actors, either, who had to somehow cling on while Ron rewrote the play, or even redesigned the production, around them.

But the people who were never exasperated or furious were

the audience. He was brilliant at it, so the audience were only ever entertained.

And that was Ron's biggest and most abiding message to me, in the short but unforgettable time that I worked with him: 'Who are you going to trust?' he once said to me in his dressing room when I'd gone to consult him about a part of our show that wasn't going well for me. 'The director or the audience?'

What he was telling me was, the audience are always the most important people in any theatre, and, especially in comedy, the audience will always let you know if what you're doing is right or wrong, or whether it works or it doesn't. So tune in to the audience and find out.

Of course, television doesn't always provide you with an audience to bounce things off – and certainly not television like *Touring Toolshed*. So you're operating on the fly there, and you know that some of the things you're coming up with will land, and some won't. But you film them and you put them out there and hope.

I'm very fond of some of the little routines that Jay and I came up with for those moments – like, for instance, the biscuit-dunking contest in the style of a spaghetti western gun duel, or the one where I'm sitting with Jay eating ice cream and having an earnest conversation, apparently oblivious to the giant blob of vanilla soft-whip clinging to my nose. They don't redefine the boundaries of comedy, but they're not supposed to. They're just there to raise a smile and gently move the show along.

And then there are the ones where I simply told Jay wince-inducing jokes.

Well, I think of them as jokes. You could call them lapses of intelligence, I suppose. Maybe it's the same thing.

What's certainly true is that some of them were so old that they were in black and white.

A judge said to a criminal in court: 'Have you been up before me before?'

And the criminal replied: 'I don't know, m'lud. What time are you usually up?'

You see, in my opinion there are jokes which are so dusty that they're funny again on account of all the dust. Well, I hope so, anyway. That's certainly the way they seem to me. Jay frequently begged to differ.

Then there was the little set-up where I teased Jay about his barrel-making skills. Though maybe I should have known from my previous experiences with mock fights that this one might come unstuck on us.

The set-up was this: having been shown how to do it by an expert, Jay was going to have a go at the tricky art of constructing a barrel using only strips of wood and hoops. Meanwhile I would sit off to one side with a mug of tea, making helpful comments such as 'We haven't got three days to make this show, you know' and 'You need to put your thumb in there' – which drew from Jay the somewhat terse response: 'I'll tell you where I'll put my thumb in a minute if you don't stop talking.'

When Jay was done, we duly graded his efforts. The barrel-making expert gave him 4 out of 10, which I thought a little generous. The way I saw it, as a barrel maker, Jay made a very good ballroom dancer. I gave him 3.

Thoroughly entering into the spirit of the scene, Jay then made a huffy and pre-planned exit.

'The two of you can do one,' he said, walking out of shot. 'I've had enough.'

Now, in the context of the show there was no way this scene could be read as anything other than panto – the kind of bantering back-and-forth that we were doing, in some form or other, at some point in every episode. Nevertheless, this being 2024, that sequence, once it went out, caused a small flurry of online headlines about Jay storming off the set.

Yes, in a way, it was me and Nick having that fake barney on the set of *Only Fools* all over again. And I should have seen it coming.

But it got even better. The following week, the programme was temporarily shifted out of its time slot to make way for a football match – which, of course, is what generally happens when big live sports events come along. Not even the slot for the news is preserved in those circumstances, so it's pretty safe to infer that there's no slight intended to any show that finds itself bumped along.

Nevertheless a highly imaginative person on a newspaper

website managed to put that innocent piece of reschedul-
ing together with the previous week's play-fight to generate
the magnificent two-hit headline: 'SIR DAVID JASON'S
SHOW PULLED OFF AIR AFTER JAY BLADES
WALKED OFF SET'.

Of course, one can laugh – clickbait is clickbait, after all,
and if you do click on the headline and read the story it very
quickly becomes apparent that you've been hoodwinked and
that there's nothing going on here at all.

But what about the people who read the headline and
don't click? What's the impression that *they* take away? That
it's gone wrong between me and Jay Blades and that the show
is getting canned?

Ah well. You shrug and move on, I guess. It's quite troubling how much nonsense is out there these days, jostling
for people's attention, and the best thing you can do, I suppose, is just try and tiptoe your way through it, because this
is where we are now.

Where I was, at least, was back on the telly. And at that
particular moment, after the dry spell induced by the pandemic, I couldn't have been happier about it. Moreover,
Marvo the Mystic, my beloved coin-operated magician
whom I'd introduced Jay to via video at our first meeting in
Sussex, made an appearance every week in the show's opening sequence. And for the final episode, Jay came to my place
and we filmed a whole segment devoted to Marvo, in which
I took the back off the cabinet and literally let light in on

the magic. (It's all done with wires, you know. No mirrors, though. Mirrors are for amateurs.)

So what a delight and a privilege that whole *David and Jay's Touring Toolshed* experience turned out to be. I'm so pleased to have had the opportunity to share a screen with the great man.

Marvo, I mean, not Jay. Although, between you and me, I'm pretty pleased I shared a screen with Jay, too.

And the show went out on dark evenings, in the deep midwinter, and if it briefly made the world seem a bit warmer for a few people, then that was all it was intended to do, and that's more than enough.

259

CHAPTER SEVEN

Of beginnings, endings and the
surprise of all surprises

Dylan Thomas's *Under Milk Wood* opens with the line: 'To begin at the beginning.'

Never a bad position from which to kick off a story, of course. As Julie Andrews has further made clear, the beginning is 'a very good place to start'.*

I've always thought of that Dylan Thomas piece as having some important associations in my life – and of being the beginning of a few things for me, in fact. But I've only recently discovered the very biggest of those associations. And the biggest of those beginnings.

I would have first heard *Under Milk Wood* in the Richard

---

* In 'Do Re Mi' in *The Sound of Music*, of course, prior to informing us about a doe being a female deer and a ray being a drop of golden sun, etc. *The Sound of Music* opened on Broadway in 1959, and *Under Milk Wood* in 1954, so Thomas wrote about the value of the beginning as a place to start five years before Rodgers and Hammerstein did.

Burton recording from 1954 – Burton reading the part for First Voice ('To begin at the beginning . . .') in that deep and rich tone of his, and Hugh Griffiths, equally charismatic, playing Captain Cat, and with Diana Maddox as Polly Garter. I was in my teens and the magic of those words and the chorus of those voices spoke very loudly to me.

In the first place, I associated the piece with the voices of my mother and her sister, my Aunt Ede, who had emigrated with her from Merthyr Tydfil to London, and who were constant – and very chatty – companions throughout my childhood. And I associated it with summer holidays staying with my relatives in the mining community of Pontlottyn in Glamorgan. Welsh voices were a dominant and resounding part of my life's soundtrack.

And then I associated it with getting under way as an actor. In 1967, Malcolm Taylor – my entrepreneurial producer friend who, you may recall from earlier, had the misguided idea of getting me to try out as a stand-up comedian – asked me to be in a production of *Under Milk Wood* that he was getting together. This was three years before that film version I talked about earlier. He knew I could do a very passable South Wales accent – I had perfected it by mimicking my cousins as a kid when I used to take the mickey out of them.

I jumped at that. This was bang in the middle of that tricky phase in the early years of my career when my one-year contract with Bromley rep had run out and I was trying to keep myself afloat with acting jobs as and when I could find them – and, as I mentioned earlier, sometimes failing and ending up back on the building sites with a screwdriver in my hand.

So, this was welcome work indeed – a week-long run at the Watermill Theatre, a lovely converted red-brick corn mill sat beside the River Lambourn, and which, as I recall, had only just opened for professional productions. Indeed, I believe our *Under Milk Wood* was the first show there with paying punters.

The Watermill Theatre still thrives, by the way. Indeed, as I write this, the place is basking in the considerable glow of having been named Theatre of the Year in the 2024 Stage Awards, sharing the prize jointly with the National Theatre in London, no less.

Also in the cast for Malcolm's *Under Milk Wood* was Ruth Madoc – except she was still going by the name Ruth Llewellyn then. Her future husband, Philip Madoc, was on board, too. Was this where they got together? It might well have been. Very lovely people, those two, and also actors with some serious range. Ruth, of course, would be rendered lastingly famous for playing Gladys Pugh in *Hi-di-Hi!*, but perhaps what people know less is that she could cut it onstage in a Sondheim musical like *Gypsy*, when she wanted to. She had a great singing voice.

Similarly, Philip reached most people's attention by being cast repeatedly in *Doctor Who* as various villainous types, and by playing the German U-boat commander who asks Corporal Pike for his name in that frequently clipped episode of *Dad's Army*.* But he was also the RSC-trained actor who played David Lloyd George in that lavish BBC drama series from the early 1980s.

When Philip died, in 2012, the very funny Welsh comic Wyn Calvin pointed out that it would be for both that Lloyd George performance and that *Dad's Army* scene that people remembered Philip, and added: 'How splendid to be remembered for something so serious and something so funny.' Amen to the possibility of that.

Another member of the cast that Malcolm assembled was an actress called Jennifer Hill. Jennifer was a little older than me – four years – but we were at very similar places in our careers. Like me, she had spent a year in rep – in her case with Wolverhampton Repertory Company – on a contract, learning the ropes and taking the roles as they came in plays like *Charley's Aunt*, *Billy Liar*, *Time to Kill*, *Dry Rot*.

And then, as with me, the security of that contract had come to an end and she had been cast out onto the open sea as a jobbing actor of no fixed production, seeking work where she could find it, and sucking it up when she couldn't.

---

* 'Don't tell him, Pike' is Arthur Lowe's immortal line at that point. This scene gets shown as frequently as the one with Victor Meldrew reaching down to pick up the phone and ending up answering a puppy, and the one with a certain person falling through a bar flap. This is honourable company to be in.

As such, for both of us, the offer of, say, a tiny bit part in a TV police series like *Z-Cars* or *Softly Softly* would have been something for which to bite off a casting director's hand. I think I marginally beat Jennifer to that *Softly Softly* benchmark, getting myself a few seconds of precious screen-time in 1966 in the role of a character unimaginatively named 'Smith'. But I know Jennifer got there too, shortly after I did – and actually played a character with the full complement of two names rather than just a surname.

Two names! That was living the dream.*

She may even have had a couple of lines to speak which, if I remember rightly, is more than I had. In my *Softly Softly* episode, all Smith had to do was get woken up from a doze in the front seat of a van.

Now, obviously, as Telly Savalas so famously reminded us in his recording of the song 'If', a picture paints a thousand words. But if you're an actor trying to get noticed, you'd rather have a couple of lines than a picture any day,

---

* Someone else with a solitary episode of *Softly Softly* under their belt: Sir Michael Gambon. Even the very greatest voyagers among us must commence their journeys somewhere – must begin at the beginning, indeed. Why, just the other day I was watching an old episode of *Heartbeat* in the company of my mother-in-law, Shirley (though known to me as Burley), when who should heave into view before our startled eyes but Benedict Cumberbatch in a younger incarnation. I refer you to the point I just made about journeys. Incidentally, my mother-in-law has a seemingly unquenchable thirst for *Heartbeat*, which I often rib her about. But between you and me, so do I. I think it's really well done.

whatever Telly Savalas has to say about it. And whichever show you're on.*

Anyway, Jennifer, Ruth, Philip and I played out our short run in Newbury, to very nice responses in the main, and all went our separate ways.

Three years later, in the spring of 1970, Malcolm Taylor decided to stage *Under Milk Wood* again, this time at the Mermaid Theatre in London. And this time it was booked for a two-month run. Ruth Madoc was in that one, too, and so was John Wayne's future favourite British sitcom star Windsor Davies.

Add me to the pile and the audiences who attended that production were watching three future stars of three big British comedy series together in one place, and all speaking in Welsh accents – quite the coincidence. But none of us were doing anything especially funny in this context, so I don't suppose anyone guessed.

Jennifer Hill also returned to the production. There's a cast photo in which we're all together in our civvies, me with my thumbs in my belt loops and wearing a cravat.

Yes, a cravat. I notice your eyebrows are up. Do you have a

---

* Telly Savalas, who played the lollipop-sucking detective Kojak, had a number-one hit with his entirely spoken version of 'If' in 1975. But yet again, I'm telling you nothing here that you don't already know. *Kojak* was even better than *Heartbeat*, I would maintain, though my mother-in-law would probably disagree.

comment to make? Trust me, it's what the wry, sophisticated man-about-town was wearing in those days.

Meanwhile Jennifer and Windsor are both sporting polo-neck jumpers, lending the picture something of the flavour of the cover for a knitting pattern, and the whole thing couldn't scream 'the sixties going into the seventies' louder if some of the members of the Beatles were in it in the background, squabbling with each other.

Anyway, during that run Jennifer and I rekindled our friendship from Newbury. The cravat worked its magic, clearly, and nature duly took its course and we ended up having a short fling.

I should say that, when it came to relationships in those days, short flings were all I seemed to be able to manage. I was so entirely focused on building my career that I fled instantly from any relationship that threatened to turn serious on me.

Relationships meant ties, you see – and not cravats: a more burdensome kind, if you can imagine such a thing. And those ties would be bound to hold me back professionally in some way. Well, that's how I saw it, anyway. And for better or worse, that would remain my attitude for many years after this – until, I guess, I had got sufficiently established that I could relax enough to think properly about fully admitting someone else into my life. And I'm so glad I did wait, because it meant I eventually found the person who was to fill that gap, the wonderful Gill who was to become my wife.

So Jennifer and I had our fling and, having flung, ceased flinging. Which, I have to say, was fine by both of us. We separated perfectly amicably, neither of us having misled the other about our intentions or where we were at in our lives. It was just a very nice interlude. A while after this I heard that Jennifer had got together with the actor Geoffrey Davion and that they were getting married. I was very happy for her and glad that she had found somebody to make a go of things with.

Meanwhile, Malcolm's *Under Milk Wood* had obviously become the production that could not be stopped. A year later, in the spring of 1971, Malcolm secured the show another revival, this time at the Unicorn Arts Theatre in London, which has since dropped the Unicorn and is now just the Arts Theatre.

Jennifer wasn't available that time, and neither was Ruth, but in came Nell Curran and Marion Grimaldi, who was rather grand and had a background in musical theatre and whole albums to her name. Still, the theatre's a great leveller and Marion and I shared the distinction of having appeared in BBC pantomimes: in the battle of the CVs, it was my *Mother Goose* with Terry Scott in 1965 versus her *Robinson Crusoe* with Norman Wisdom a couple of years later. Let's call it a draw.

Even then, it wasn't over for Malcolm's unstoppable *Under Milk Wood*, which duly rolled on to Sadler's Wells Theatre for a further week that October. And this time it was my turn to be unavailable, having moved on to better things – or, at any rate, having moved on to a more substantial booking which would end up keeping me off the streets a bit longer.

Specifically, I had landed the part of Paul in a touring production of a farce by Richard Harris called *Partners*. Blackpool, Cardiff, Weston-super-Mare, Bradford, Nottingham, Brighton, Hull . . . Dear reader, courtesy of *Partners*, I behaved farcically in all of those great British locations that autumn and winter, enjoyed the warmth of their people's welcome, and also knew the glory of the nylon bedsheets in their very cheapest guest houses.

For such was touring in that halcyon period for the strolling player that I had become: a train journey to a strange town, a week of anxious and fretful nights in electro-statically charged bedding, followed by a congealed fried egg in the breakfast room, and away to the next stop. How we all coped with the sheer six-star glamour of it all, I have no idea.

My co-star in that production of *Partners*, by the way, was Peter Adamson, who famously went on to be Len Fairclough in *Coronation Street*. But the Richard Harris who wrote the play wasn't the great Irish actor whom you may know from films as far-flung as *This Sporting Life*, *Gladiator* and the *Harry Potter* series. This Richard Harris was the extremely august British screenwriter.

What I couldn't have anticipated, of course, as I lay very still for fear of igniting myself between those sheets in Blackpool, Cardiff, etc., was that, away in the future, I would again be acting out scripts penned by Richard – in *The Darling Buds of May*, for which he wrote four episodes, and *A Touch of Frost*, for which he wrote five.

Not that knowing any of this would have decreased the threat of fire damage to my bodily hair between those sheets – but I might have slept a little more soundly, nonetheless, for knowing that it would all work out OK in due course.

In between those Malcolm Taylor productions, I had, you will recall from earlier, along with Ruth, decamped to the Welsh coast for a couple of weeks to take a role in the film version of *Under Milk Wood* that came out in 1973 and so mysteriously failed to springboard me to the glittering heights of Hollywood. Those wonderful Dylan Thomas phrasings really did ring repeatedly and resonantly through my life in those days.

And they would do again.

* * *

'To begin at the beginning.'

That was how the letter began – the most astonishing letter I've ever received.

'To begin at the beginning,' the letter said. 'Well actually, at *my* beginning. I wonder whether it has ever crossed your mind, as it has done with Mum and more recently with me, that you might be my biological father?'

I was standing in the kitchen when I read this and . . .

well, shocked doesn't really begin to convey it. The letter went on:

> For a considerable time, I have wrestled with the unsettling discovery that my paternity is uncertain.
>
> I don't want Mum to feel guilty. I didn't want to 'betray' my late father and I have worried endlessly about how on earth to approach you. However, I really would like to know.
>
> I am not asking for financial support, or for you to make any other kind of commitment to me.
>
> Please would you agree to take an anonymous paternity test so that I can finally know the truth and let the matter rest?
>
> Obviously, this remains entirely between you and me.
>
> I am sorry if this sounds rather abrupt but I am trying desperately hard not to waffle. Written explanations would go on for pages, so please could we talk?

The letter was signed 'Love and best wishes, Abi x (Jenny Hill's daughter!)'

You will be unsurprised to learn that my hands were shaking by now. What had I just read? I had to go back and read the whole thing again. And then I had to read it again. And then again after that.

I have to say that it really *hadn't* crossed my mind that Abi Hill was my daughter – that my relationship with Jennifer Hill while we were in that production of *Under Milk Wood* in 1970 could have produced a child without me knowing about it.

271

At no point in the nearly fifty years that had gone by since then had that thought had cause to enter my head. It was only crossing my mind for the first time now, reading this letter, in a bewildering cascade of emotions that seemed to include everything from wonder and amazement, through anxiety and heartache, to fear and outright panic.

I knew that Jennifer and Geoffrey had a daughter – a daughter, indeed, who had followed them into the business and become an actor. That much I knew.

But that was *their* daughter, surely. That couldn't be *my* daughter . . .

Could it?

Of course, the first person I needed to share this letter with was Gill. She was initially as stunned and as discombobulated as I was. But the more we thought about it and talked about it, and the more we read and reread the letter and absorbed what it was telling us, the more we reached the same overriding emotion about it: sympathy for Abi – for this woman who had obviously been going through a turmoil of uncertainty about her parentage, and had been doing so for a long time, clearly, yet who had conveyed it so warmly and so sweetly in that letter.

So naturally I should agree to do the test. And if the test came back positive, then we should meet Abi and open our arms to her. I am so grateful that Gill was so supportive and understanding about it all.

And in any case, the test would reveal that there was no

connection between us, wouldn't it? That's what I thought, the more I considered it, in the days leading up to the test. It all just seemed so unlikely.

When the result came back, I got in touch with Abi and said, 'I think we'd better get together, don't you?'

We decided to meet on neutral ground at first, in a hotel in London. And in she walked, my almost 50-year-old daughter, the daughter I didn't know I had.

I don't think at first either of us knew quite what to do with ourselves. I struggle to describe what it's like, meeting someone you don't know at all, who is at the same time your own. I've never experienced such a jumble of competing emotions. We were both feeling them. There was a lot of elation – kind of 'Can you believe it?' and 'What an amazing thing!'

But there was an inevitable sense of distance too, and a pang of sadness for those missing years, all that lost time. So strange to feel this instant intimacy between the two of you, this obvious bond, and, at the same time, to be aware of this gap between you: so much common ground, and yet all that ground uncovered.

I held Sophie straight after she was born, and I fed her and changed her and walked her to school and watched her grow, and all of those things. And that's what I think of when I think of Sophie being my daughter. But Abi and I, of course, never had that chance, which is sad in itself, and now here she was, entering my life for the first time, but as

a grown woman. In those first minutes it was such a complicated thing to process, for us both.

But we talked, me, Abi and Gill, and Abi told us her
story. How she had spent her childhood believing that the
father who was raising her, Geoffrey Davion, was also her
birth father. How doubts about that had only begun to creep
in many years after Geoffrey died, in 1996. How she knew
that her mother and I had been together briefly around what
could have been the time of her conception. How a friend
of hers had mentioned to her, almost as a joke, that she and
I had very similar-shaped noses – and how Abi had thought:
well, hang on – yes, actually we *do*.

And Abi told us about how her mother hadn't been able to
confirm anything, but hadn't been able to rule it out, either.
And how Abi had for a long time done her best to live with
not knowing the truth, but ultimately came to realise that
she really would like to know, if it were possible – not just
for her own sake but also for the sake of her son.

Yes, a son – a ten-year-old boy named Charlie.

So, a daughter I didn't know I had, and a first grandson I
didn't know I had.

The family suddenly seemed to be expanding at quite
a lick.

We had waited to tell Sophie at what we thought was the
right time for her. She was used to being referred to as my
only daughter and I was worried about her reaction. I wanted
to speak to her on my own and so I took her off into the TV

room and sat her down and told her 'my story' – something that happened a long time ago. She took it all in, and then said, in a triumphant way: 'So, wait – I've got a sister?'

She showed so much wisdom and understanding beyond her years and, needless to say, Gill and I were relieved and thankful that she had taken it in her stride and was happy to meet these new people in her life. Abi is lovely, bright and kind, and so she too understood the unusual nature of the situation we all found ourselves in, and wanted Sophie to feel comfortable with her new sister. So, all in all, I am proud of them both.

It was nearly Christmas, so we invited Abi and Charlie over. It was lovely: nerve-racking in anticipation, I can't deny, but then lovely when it happened. I took Charlie out to the hens to fetch the eggs. And then I showed him round the workshop. Not just anybody gets permission to step inside the hallowed workshop, you know. But he was family, so he was allowed.

I call Charlie 'the Hair' because he's got quite the quantity of it – an unfair quantity of it, I would say, from my position at the, shall we say, thinner end of the spectrum.

Think of me now on these occasions, won't you? I've got Sophie's boyfriend, the BFG, making a mockery of me for height, and now I've got Charlie, the Hair, making a mockery of me for male-pattern baldness – or, as I prefer to think of it, male-pattern thinning.

Life's not getting any more dignified for me around here.

Anyway, that was Christmas. We've got together numerous times since then – Gill, Sophie, Abi, Charlie and me – and that's what we'll keep doing. It's early and there's a lot of ground to go over, for all of us. I'm getting to know Abi, and she's getting to know me, and it's going to take time. But time is what we're going to give it and we'll do it, in so far as we can manage it, in private because that's the way we'd prefer it.

Unfortunately, the newspapers had different ideas when a journalist turned up on Abi's doorstep in 2023 asking her to elaborate on the 'story' that some kind friend had put their way that I was her father. She flustered her way through a conversation, stonewalling as best she could and saying things like 'I couldn't possibly comment', and then rang me in quite a state.

A day or two later the same journalist turned up on our doorstep, so we knew the hunt was on. We always knew the day would come when our cherished privacy would go out the window. And we didn't want to ignore this approach for fear that the wider press would then get on the trail and hound us further and maybe end up producing an unsympathetic or even sordid account of the situation. So we arranged to give the full story to the journalist who made that first approach – and who, in fact, handled the situation with an understanding that we hadn't thought would be possible. So that's why you might have first read about this personal situation courtesy of an 'unnamed source'.

Jenny, Abi's mother, died in the summer of 2023, I'm sad to say. I very much hope that she was relieved to know that Abi had finally learned the truth of her beginning and that Jenny could rest in peace.

Meanwhile, though, there's another *Under Milk Wood*-related twist that's emerged. You'll remember Malcolm Taylor's seemingly indestructible stage production of the piece. Well, in 2008, forty-one years after that first shot at it in Newbury, Malcolm brought the show back yet again – this time for a fortnight at the Tricycle Theatre in London.

I was busy on *A Touch of Frost* at the time, so I couldn't appear, but I recorded the voice of the Guidebook, which was played in the production. Philip Madoc from the original cast appeared again, and so did Jennifer Hill.

And so, as Polly Garter, did Abi Hill, Jennifer's daughter – and, as it turns out, my daughter.

So there were the three of us – mother, daughter and father, had we but known it – on the same stage, albeit with one of us there in virtual form, indisputably linked together once again by the mighty words of Dylan Thomas.

Anyway, now Abi and I are finally in each other's lives – with a lot of catching up to do. Indeed, more than fifty years' worth.

We're beginning at the beginning, you could say. And Julie Andrews is right: it's a very good place to start.

EPILOGUE

Of crucial matters, flower buds and fond farewells

A low sun casts its thickening shadows across the Jason Towers lawns. A horse whinnies distantly from the re-felted stable block (excellent work, Daphne), and a reflective silence descends upon the house, broken only by the scratching of my nib and, from the butler's scullery, the faint but unmistakable sound of Strobes buttering his evening crumpet.

Yes, as the day fades this volume draws inevitably to its close, and the time for fond farewells is nigh. Yet I find that my head is wistfully abuzz with the many important questions that I had hoped to engage with in these pages but which the time and space available to us have not in the end allowed.

Questions such as: by the time the HS2 railway development is finished, will we even be travelling by train? At current rates of progress, you would have to fancy someone to have developed remote-controlled personal flight by

279

then, aerial taxis picking you up from home and dropping you directly at your destination, rendering the entire HS2 project a multi-billion-pound museum piece at the point of its ribbon-cutting.*

And questions such as: will global warming ultimately make Love Island uninhabitable? And if so, how soon, please?

And particularly questions such as: is it really possible to watch television with the fullness of attention which it (sometimes) deserves, and be on your mobile phone at the same time? Because my daughter Sophie clearly believes it is, while I confess that I struggle with the concept.

Just the other week we were watching the rugby. Well, when I say *we* were watching it, I mean *I* was watching it, while Sophie divided her attention in the usual manner.

'Blimey, look at the teeth on that bloke,' I heard her say, looking up from her phone a little distractedly, I felt.

'Sophie,' I replied, 'he's wearing a gum shield.'

We may be due a reckoning, I fear, with regard to the widespread impact on our attention spans of 'multi-tasking', to give it its formal name, and of the mobile phone in general.

Yet the discussion of this and other equally weighty matters will have to await another opportunity. For, I am gratified

---

* HS2 is currently ripping holes in some very beautiful passages of countryside round my way, so if you detect some personal animus just beneath the surface of this particular gag, you are more than welcome to.

to say, the diary is again filling up (not the *Sunday Telegraph* Gardener's one, the one on Gill's computer) and I must now set down my pen, rise from my desk and heed its calls.

What a relief to realise that the work hasn't dried up after all. And what an even greater relief to realise that I haven't dried up with it. And, with the usual caveats, some of the projects currently before me look very promising indeed. I had grown concerned in that period of recovery after the pandemic that I was now officially subject to the law of diminishing parts. It seemed to me for a while that I was destined from this moment to get offers to appear in things – but only very briefly.

'We'd only need David for two days.' That was a sentence I grew used to hearing.

Or, 'We'd only need David for a day and a half.'

And most worrying of all, 'We'd only need David for an hour or so.'

That last one, incidentally, seemed to be offering me the chance to walk up the path from a church and say 'Good morning' to someone. That was to be the sum total of my contribution to this drama, as things stood.

I mean, I suppose I've done less in my time. (I refer you back to a certain *Softly Softly* appearance, mentioned in the previous chapter.) But not that much less.

Now, I appreciate that a person should always be grateful for small mercies, and that, as we used to say on *Only Fools*, it's better than a kick up the bot from Bobby Charlton.

281

But it would be nice in general to see a few more proper parts going to the older actor, wouldn't it? And I don't just mean replacement hips. So maybe there's some campaigning to be done.

Roy Clarke had a great idea not long ago for a comedy series about a village where an entrepreneur has decided to come in with his bulldozers and build some kind of money-making monstrosity to the detriment of the neighbourhood. And the oldies in the village form a vigilante group who creep around sabotaging this building project to the best of their abilities.

I thought it had a lot going for it, yet Roy couldn't get it away. In a better world, I think he would have done. And who knows, with the right kind of campaigning, perhaps he eventually will.

Meanwhile, in addition to discussions ongoing regarding significant dramatic opportunities, there lies ahead of me another *Only Fools and Horses* convention. It took me a while to succumb to the allure of those occasions, for reasons which I talked about earlier. But now I eagerly look forward to them, and to the chance to move among the show's remarkable and ever-loyal fans and hear their tales.

And here's a thing: from where I'm sitting – or at least if I stand on the windowsill, lean out and strain quite a lot – I can make out the branches of my mighty grapefruit tree, hand-reared from a pip and now nodding nobly in its earthenware pot.

And, dear reader, you would not believe the abundance of the flower buds this year. It's speckled like a Christmas tree with them. Never has that grapefruit yielded buds in such profusion and I take this to be a highly encouraging omen.

Life is unfailingly surprising – I've learned that in no small measure these past few years. But in many ways that's been the tale of my whole life. Things move on and develop, often rather wonderfully, and either way, the art is to move on and develop with them, as who knows what's in store for any of us. If we can meet triumph and disaster and treat those two imposters just the same, we're onto a winner, as Del Boy would say.

So, on with the journey, then. Why, this time next year . . .

ACKNOWLEDGEMENTS

To all the wonderful staff at my local Hartwell House Hotel for providing a quiet corner whilst writing this and my other books.

INDEX

289